John Dough and the Cherub

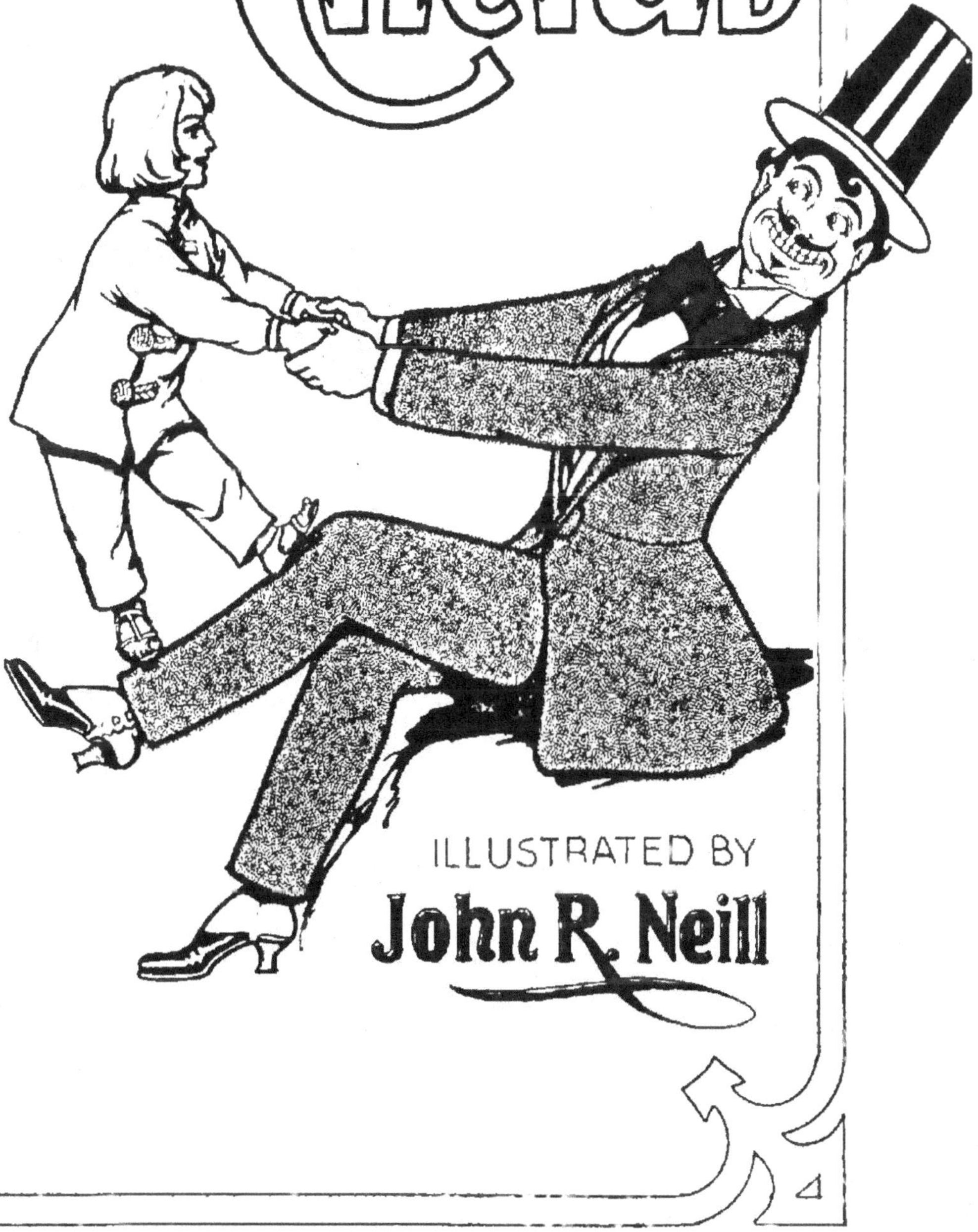

ILLUSTRATED BY

John R. Neill

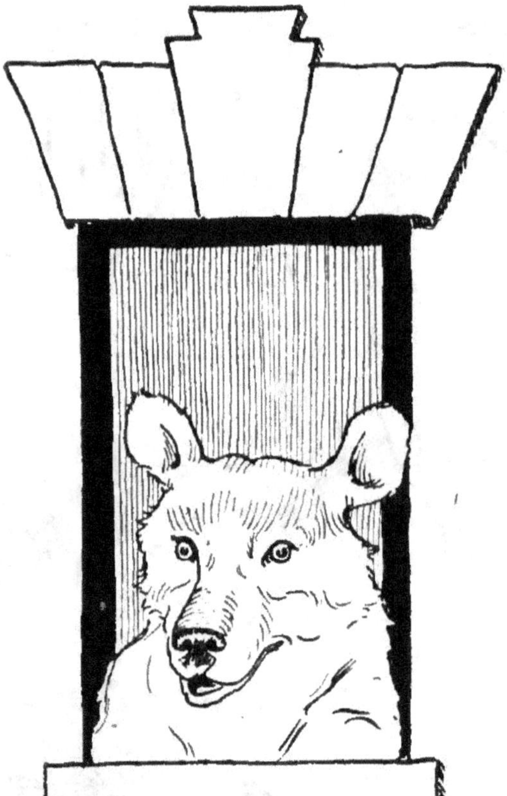

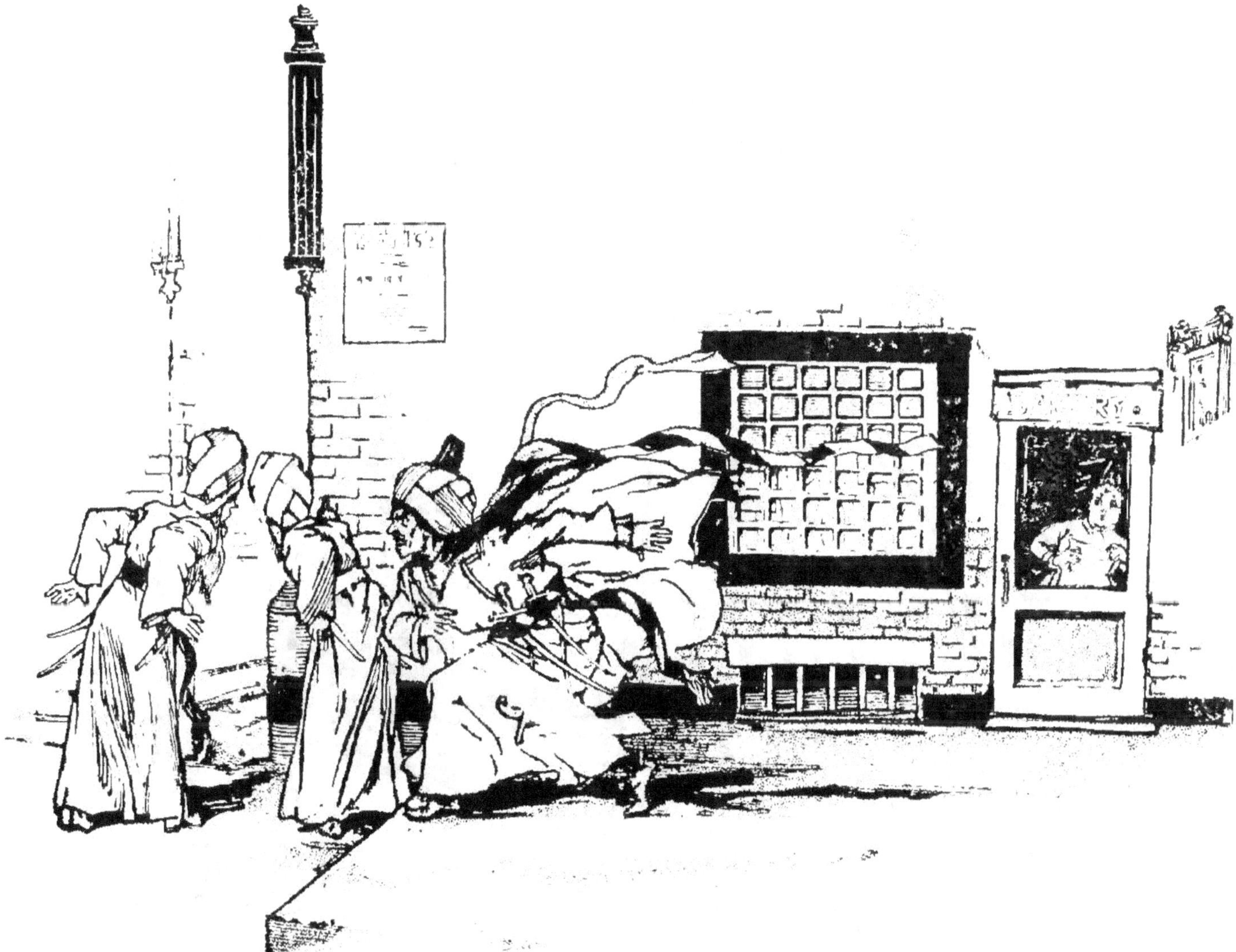

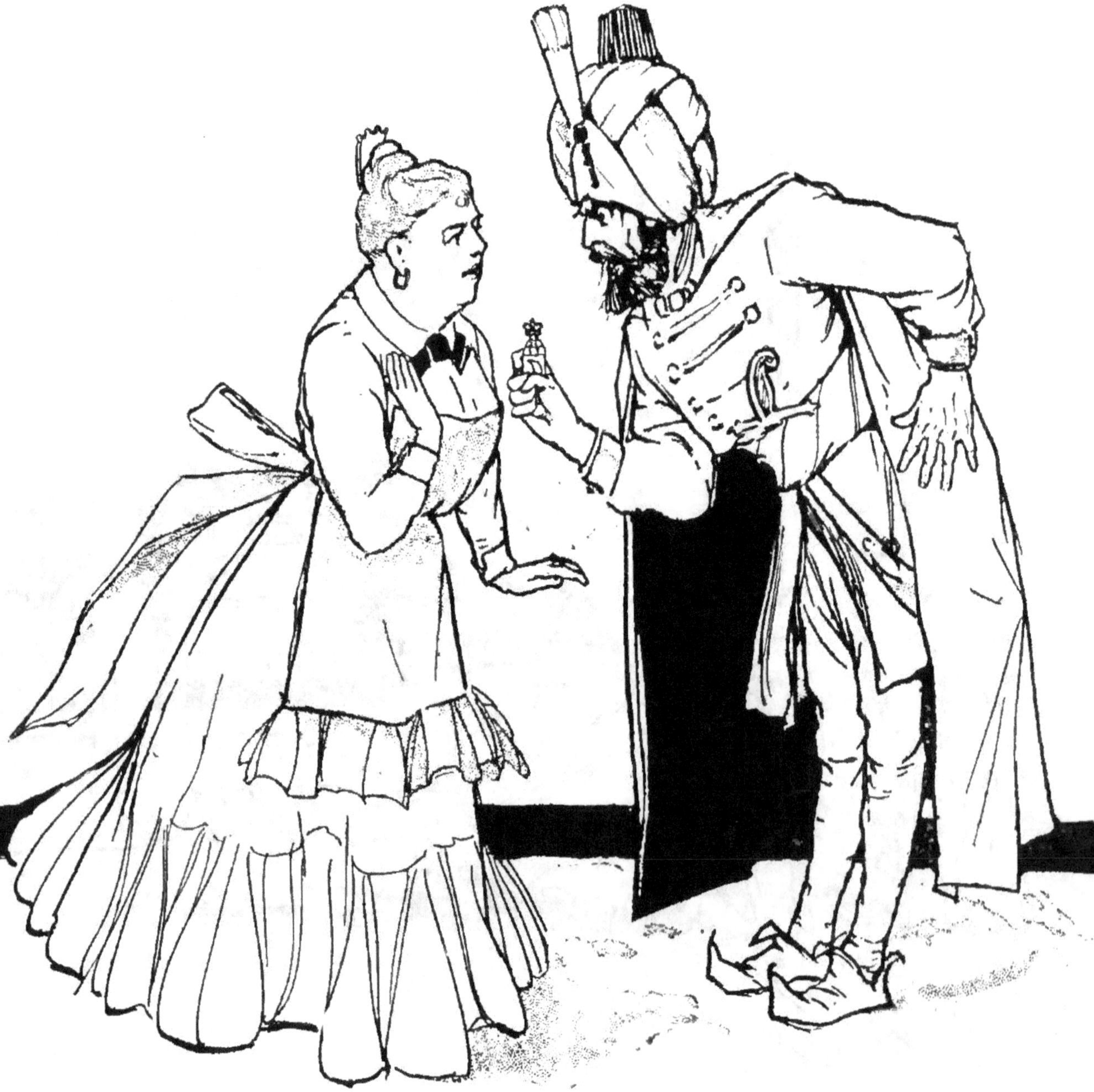

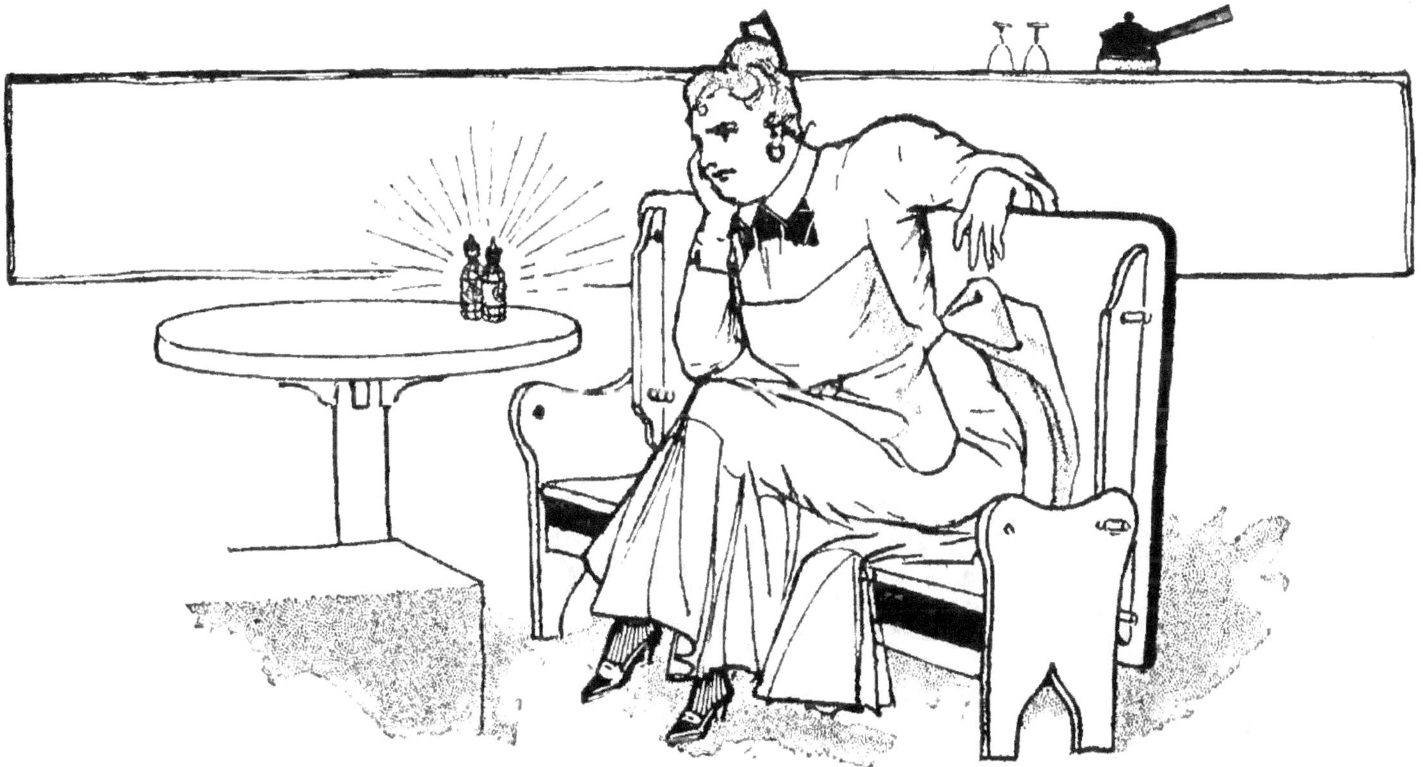

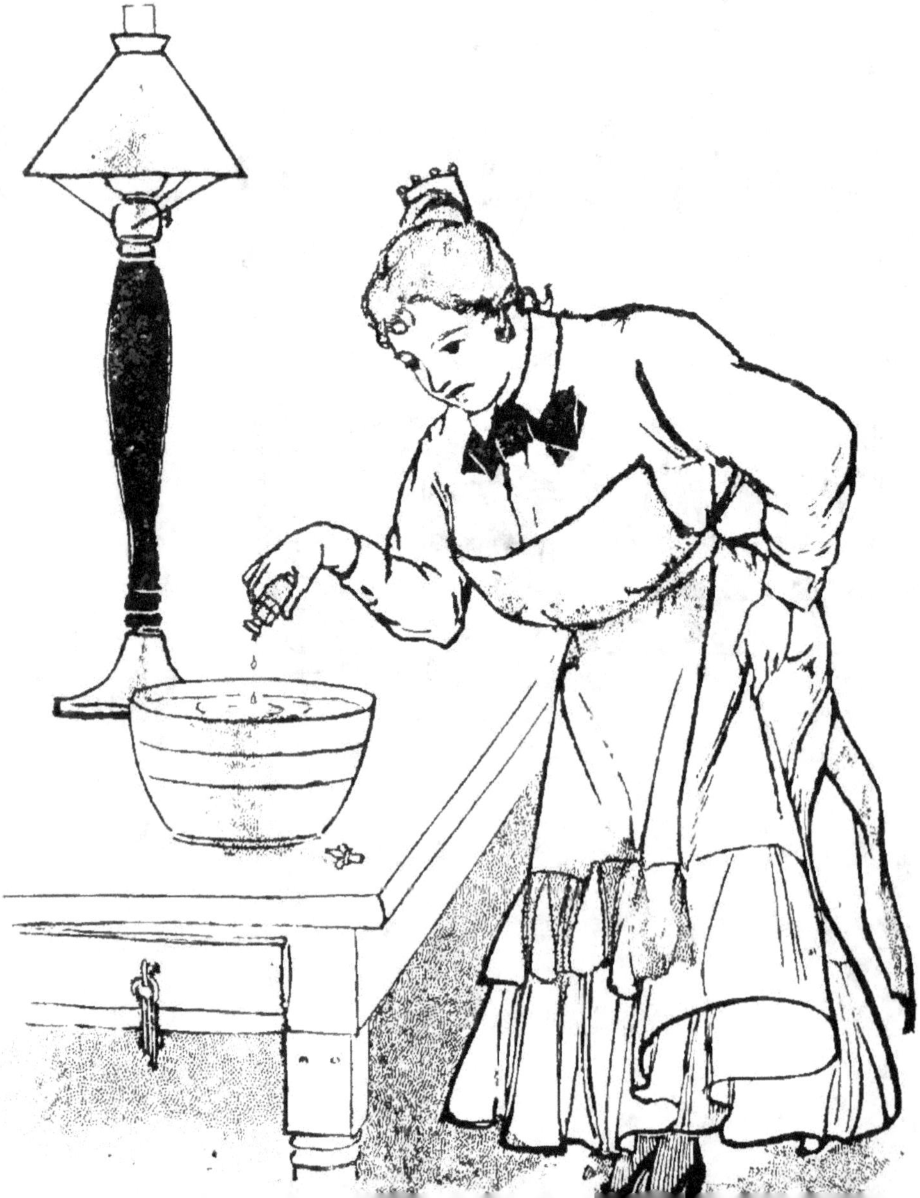

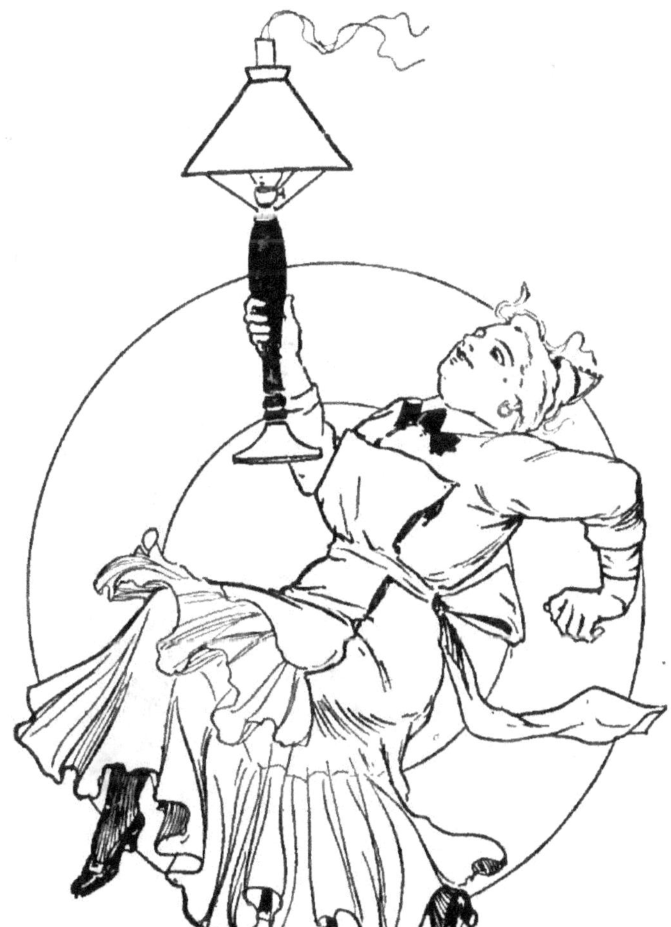

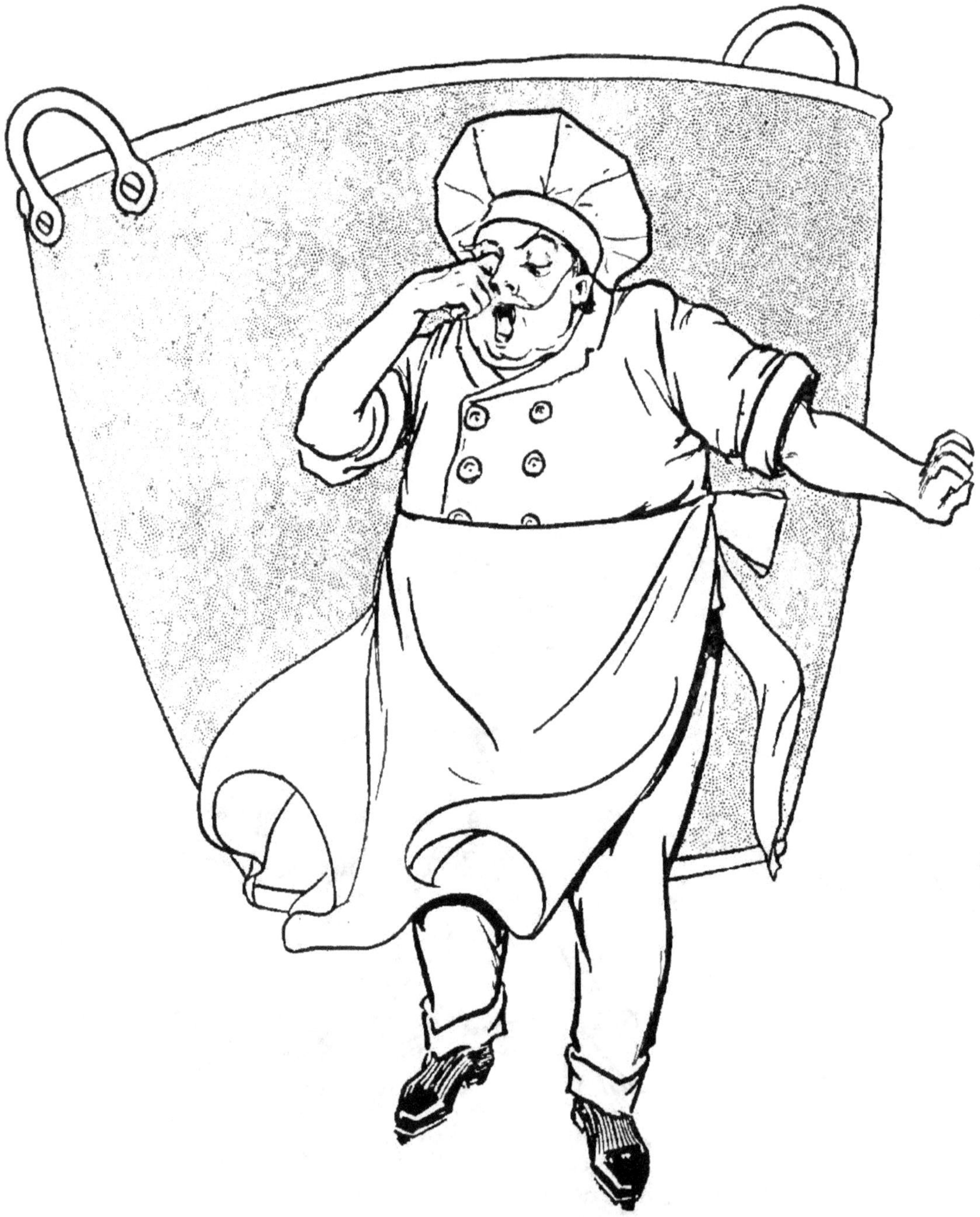

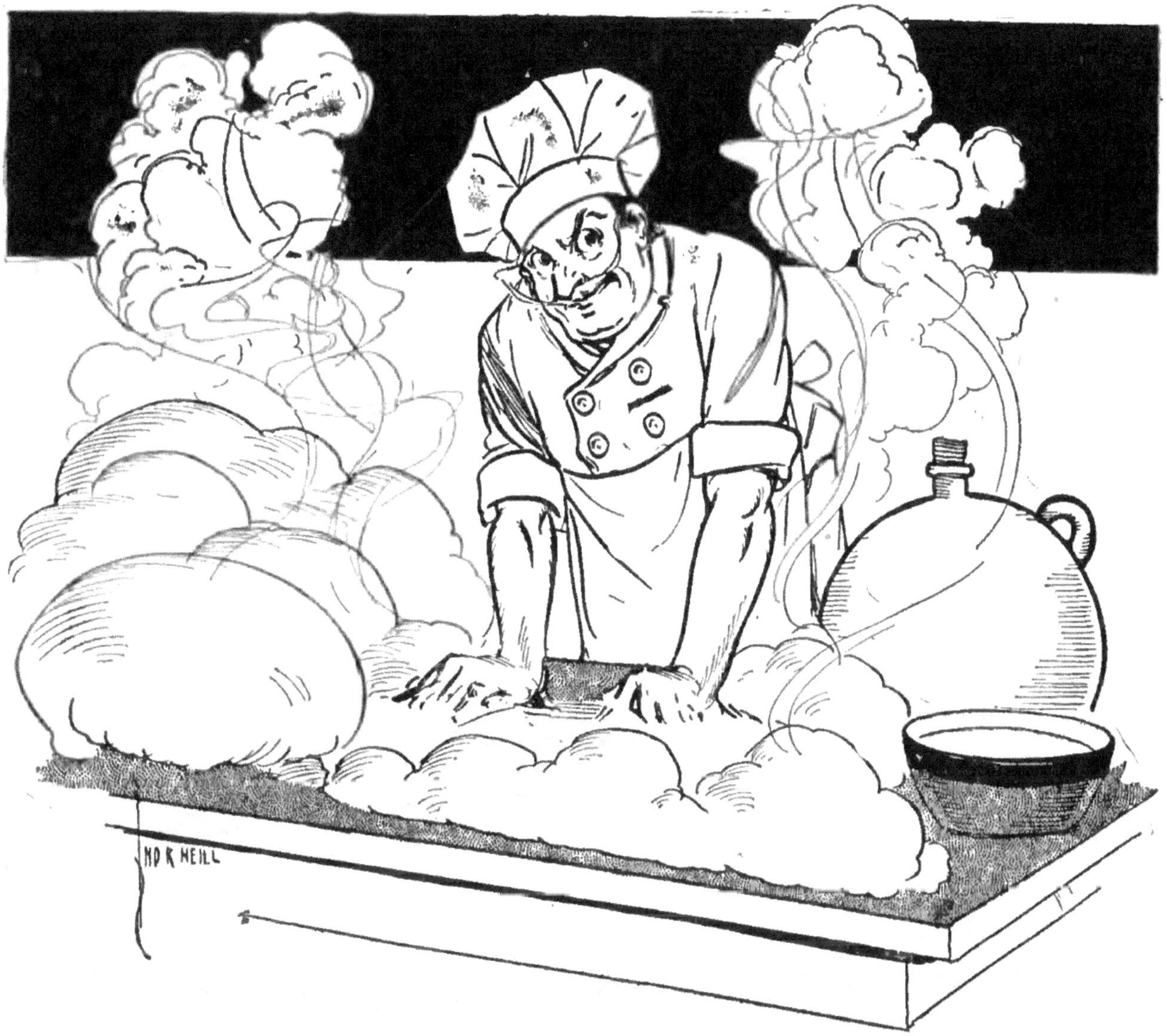

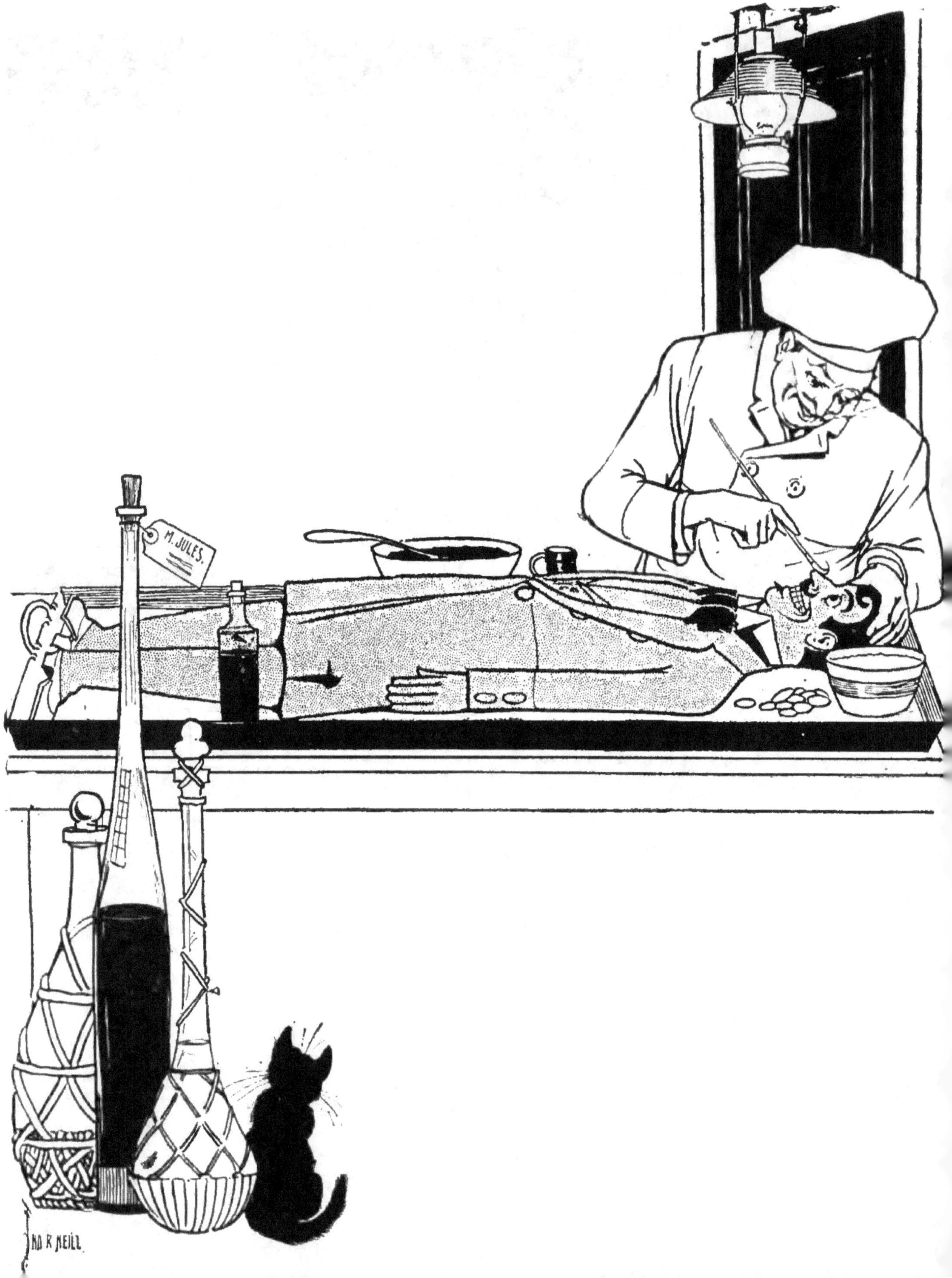
M. JULES.
JNO R. NEILL

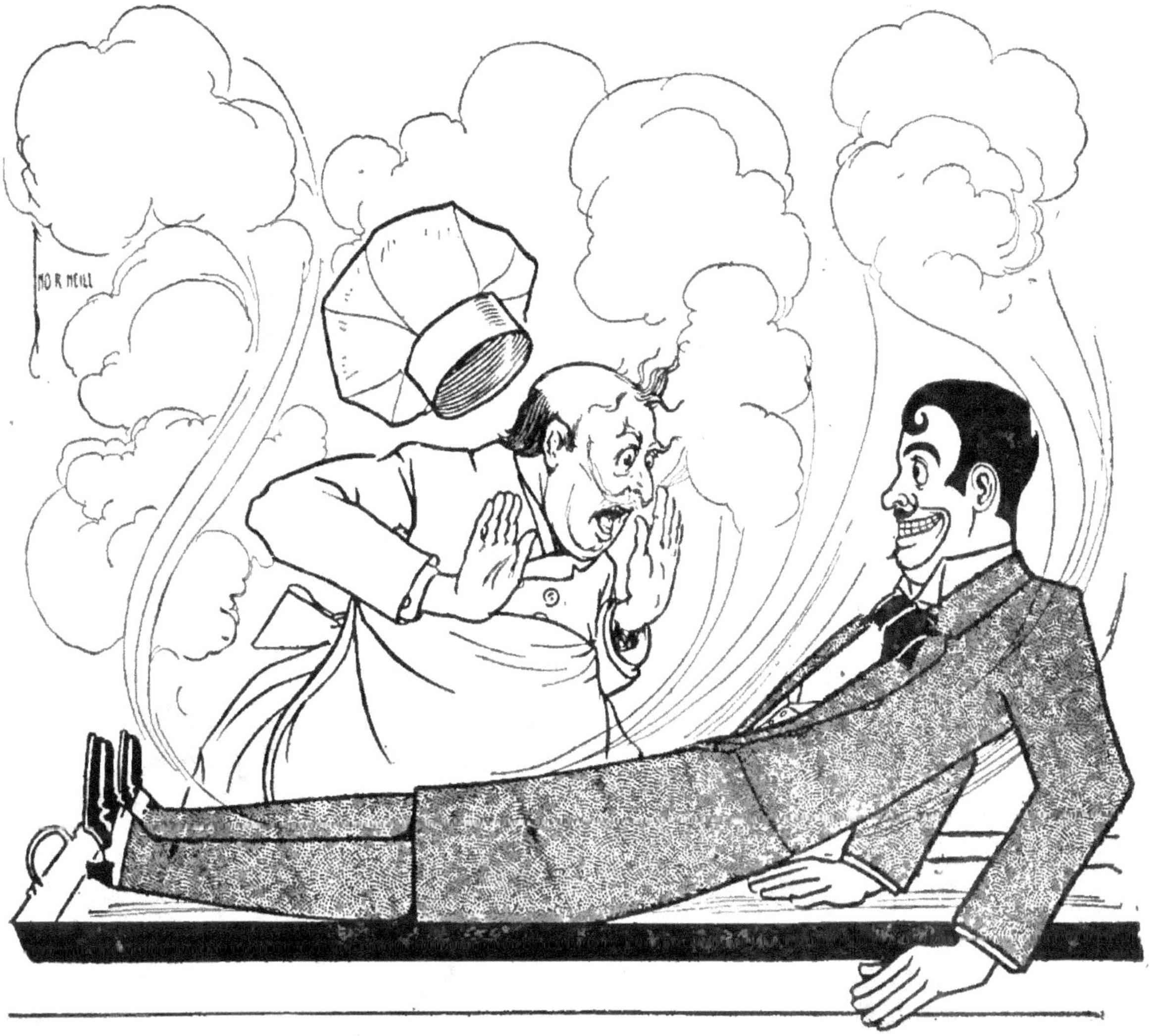
JNO R NEILL

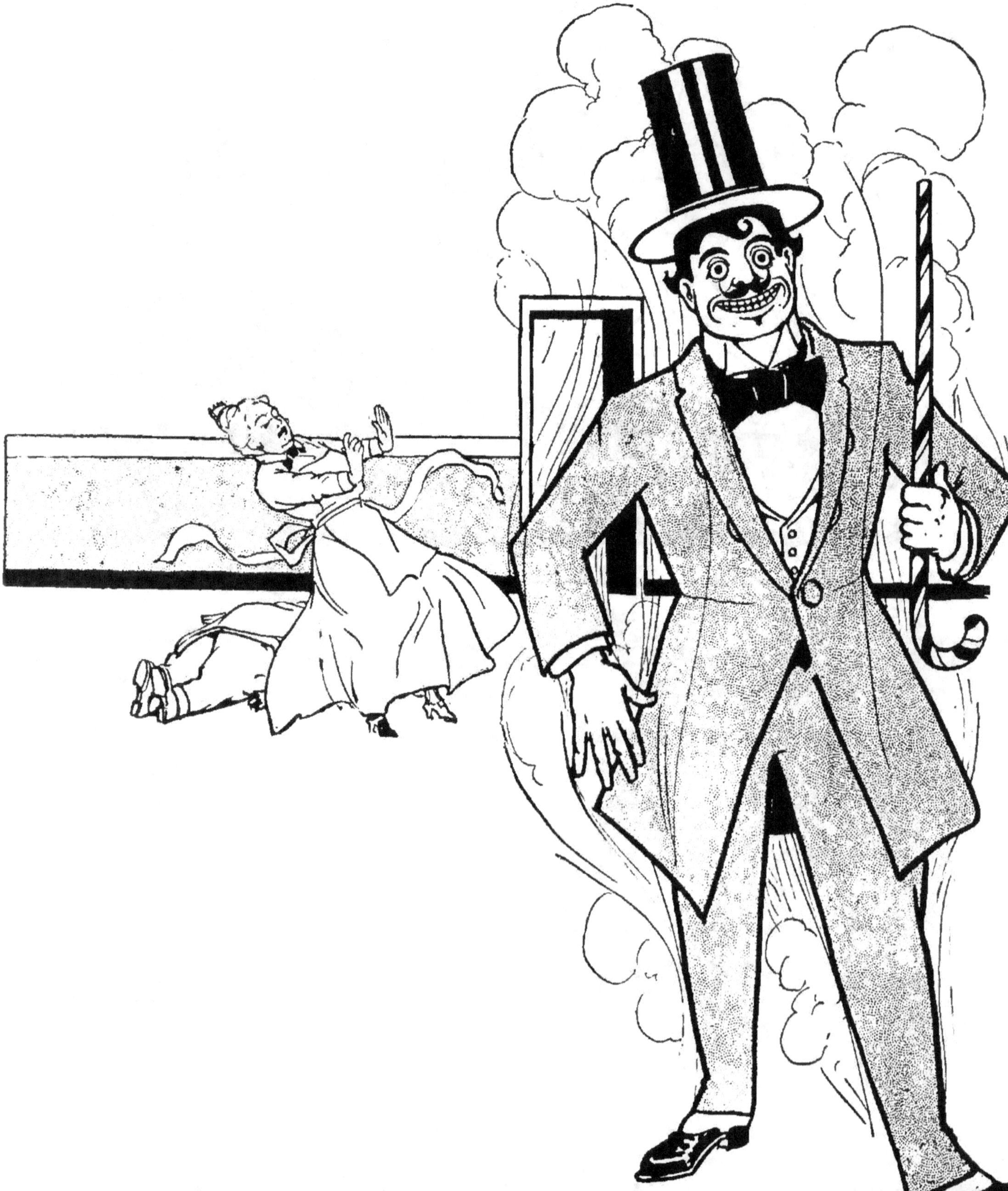

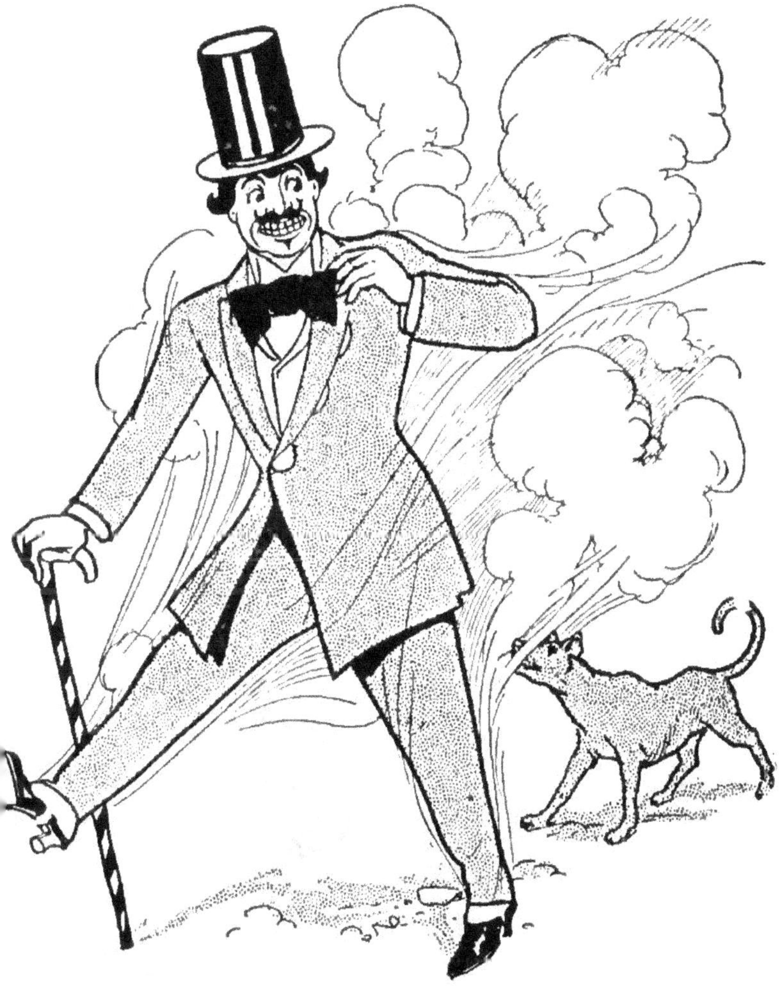

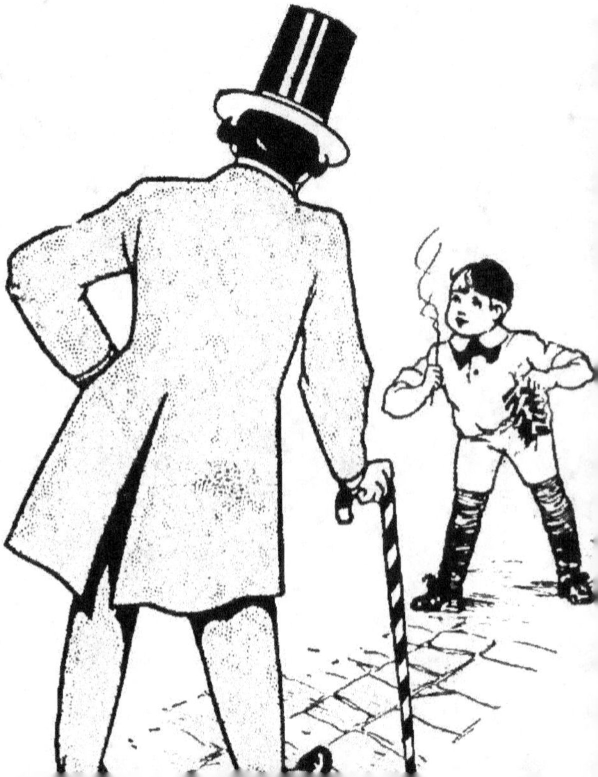

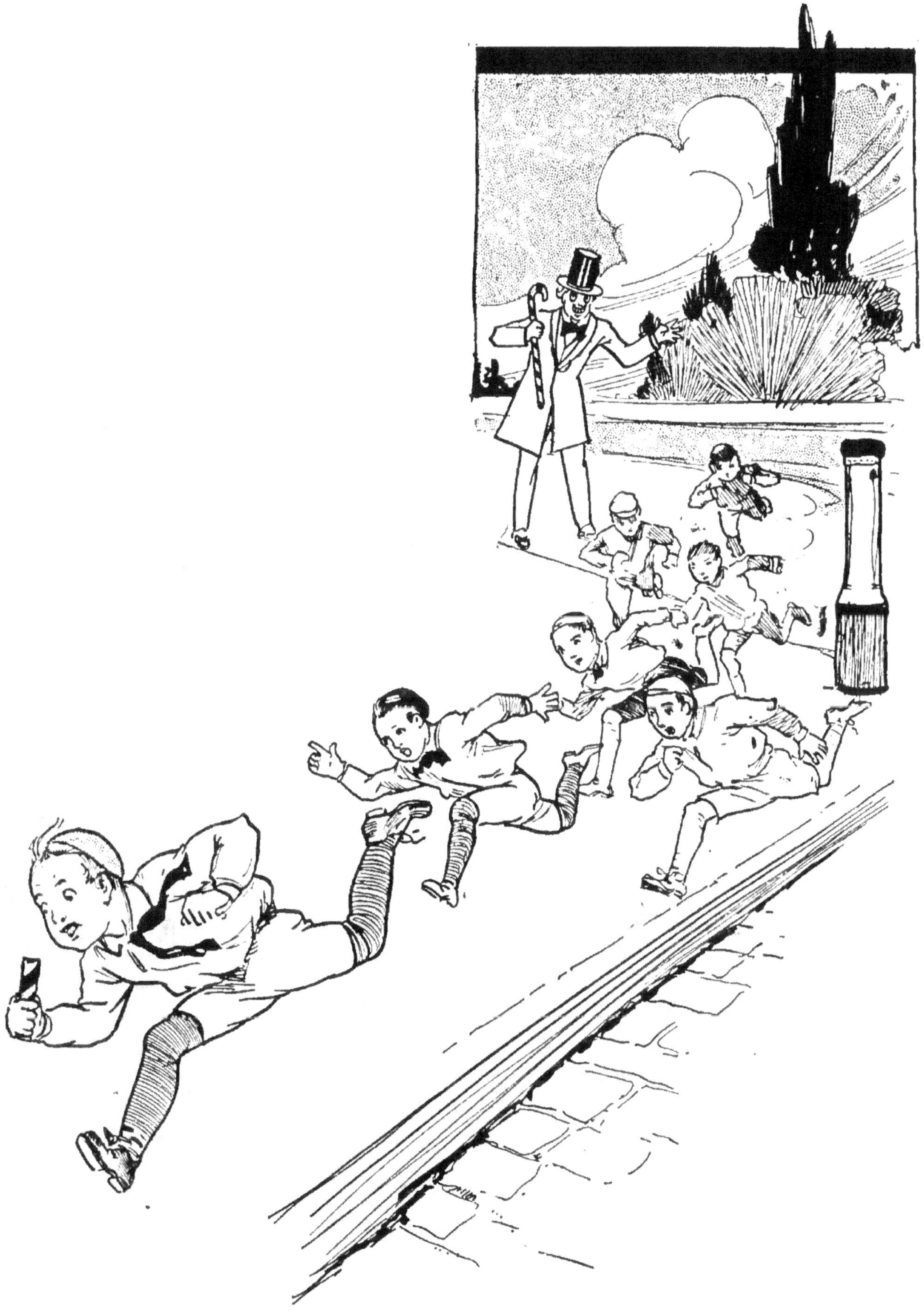

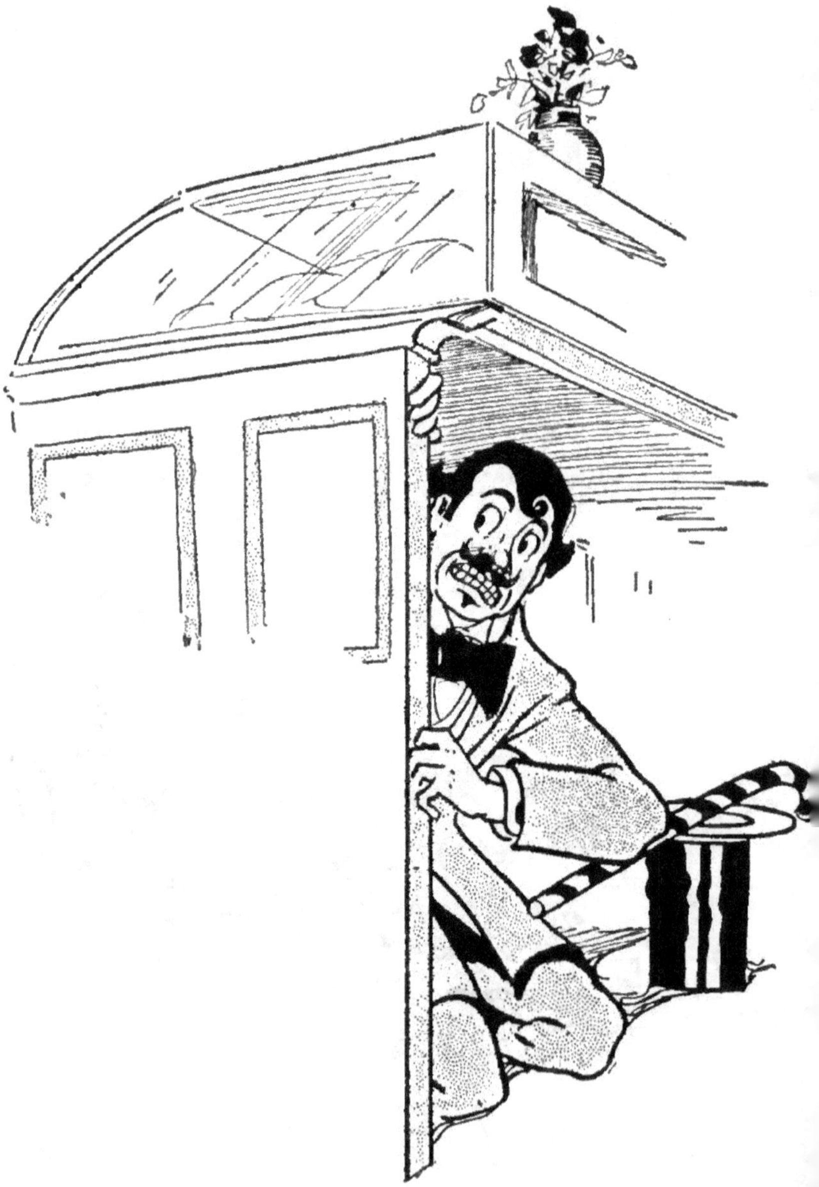

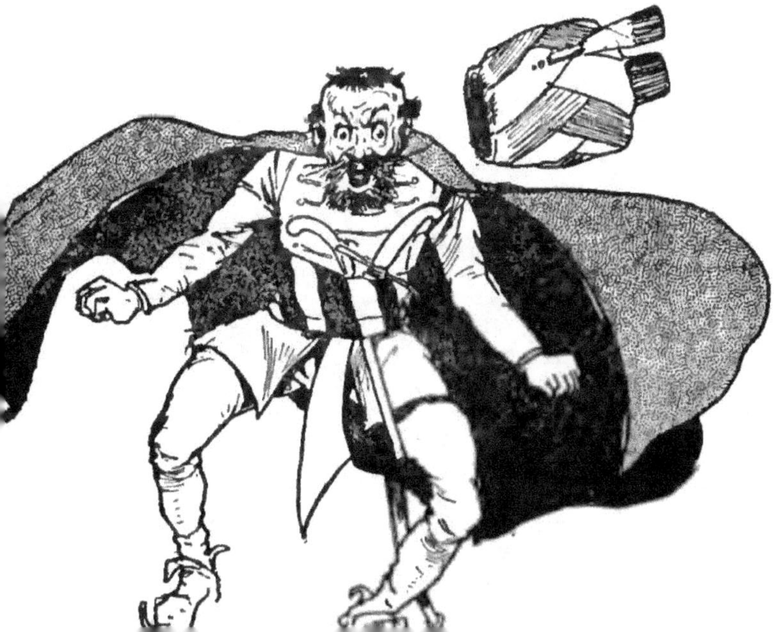

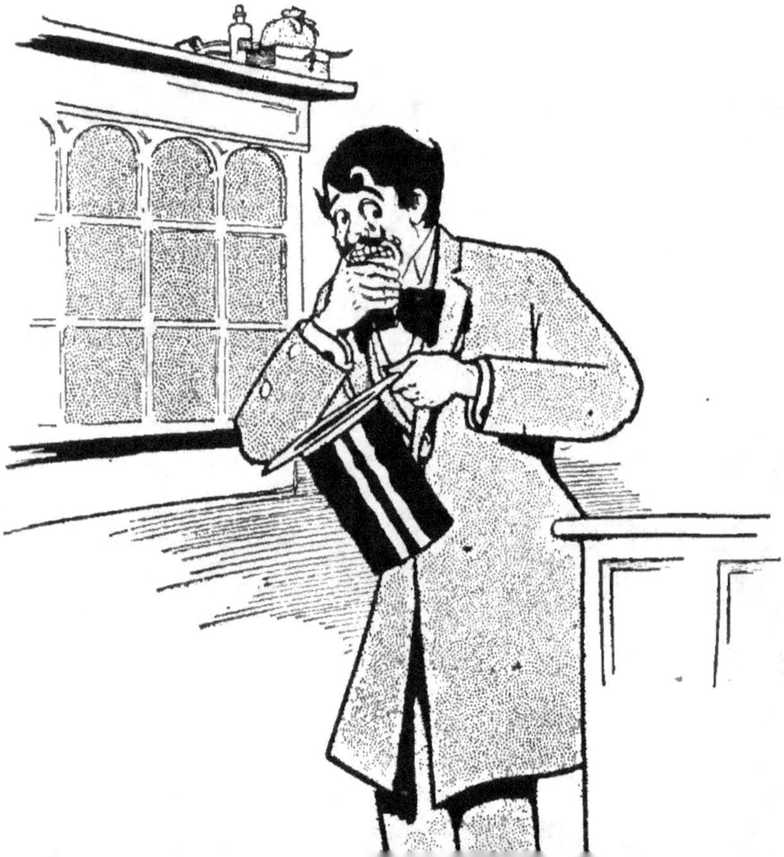

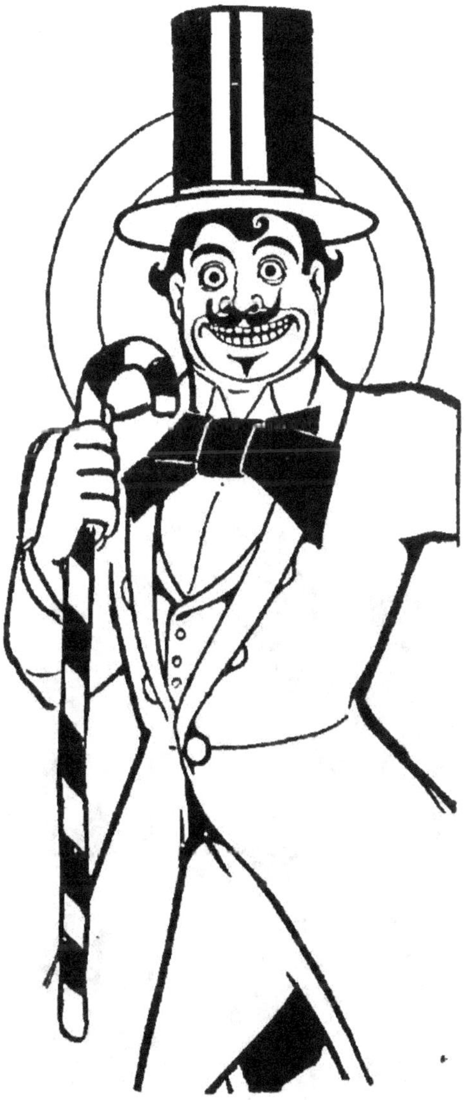

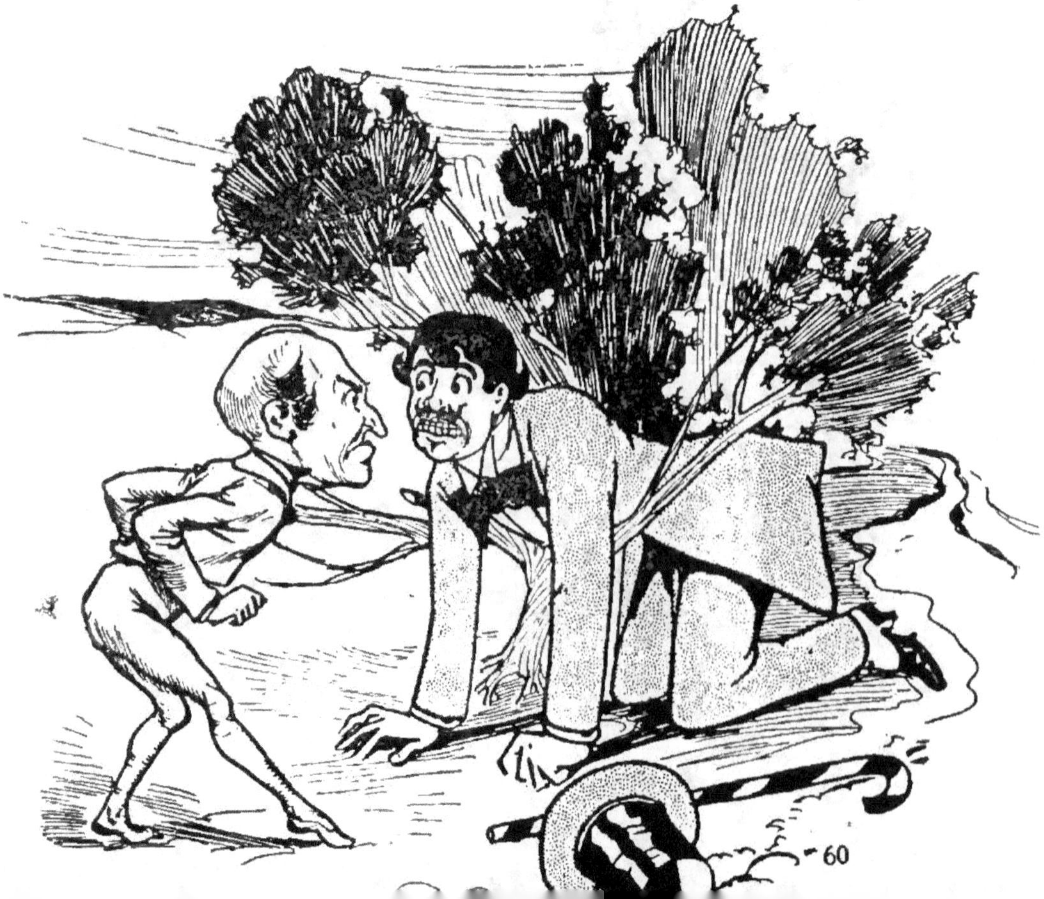

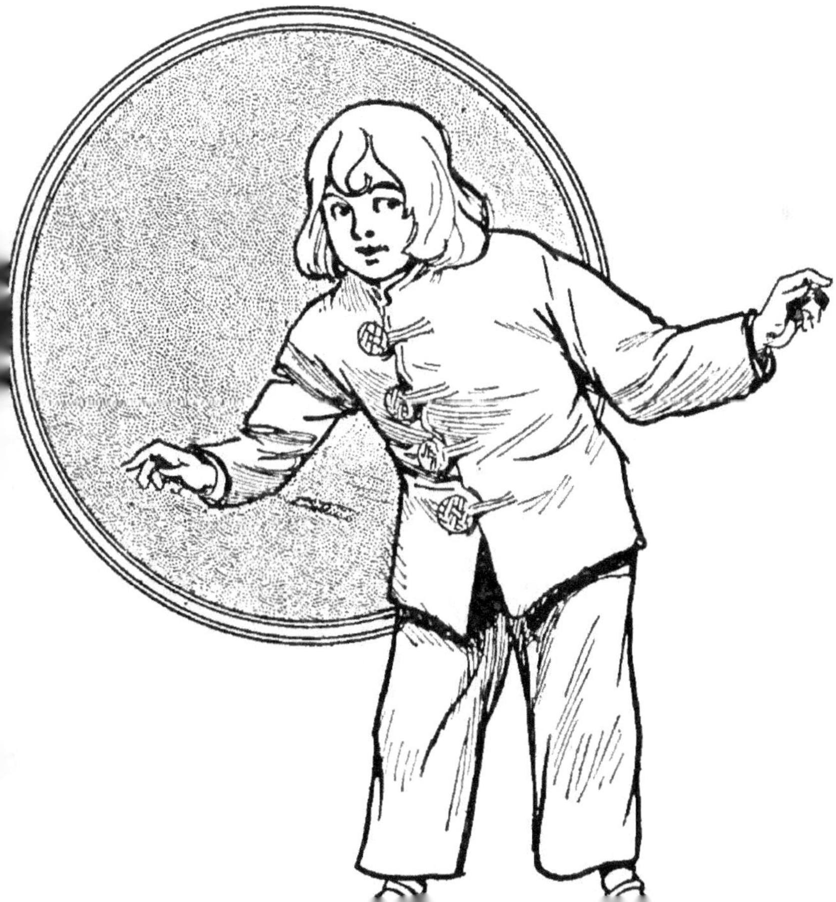

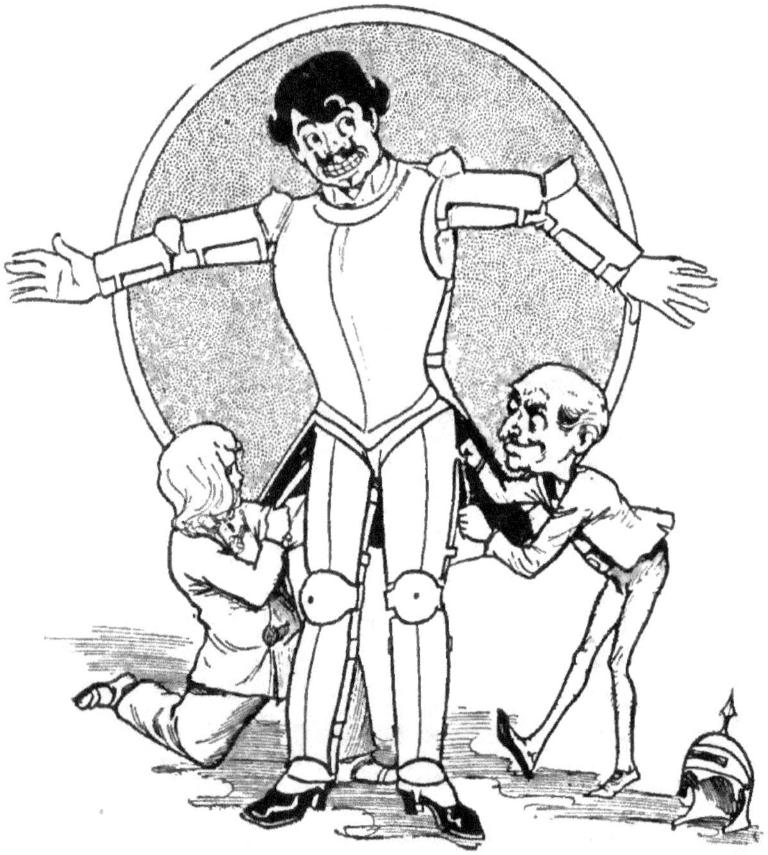

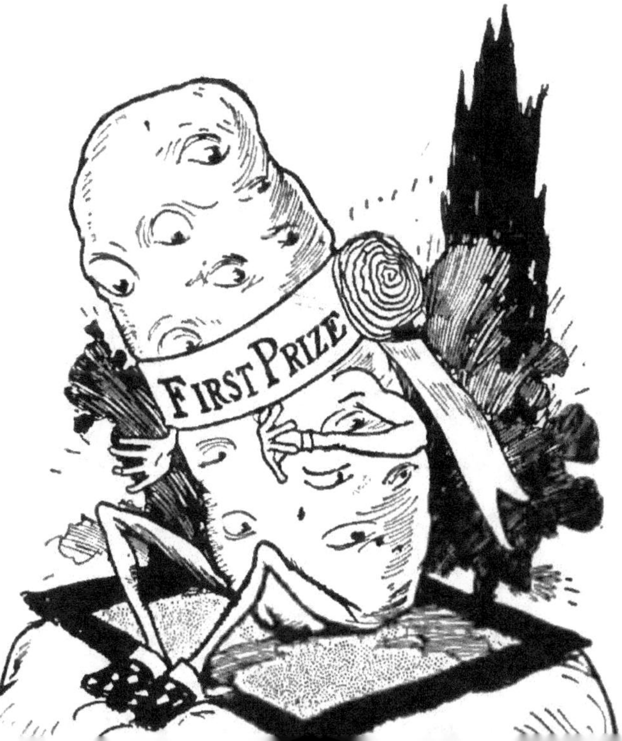
FIRST PRIZE

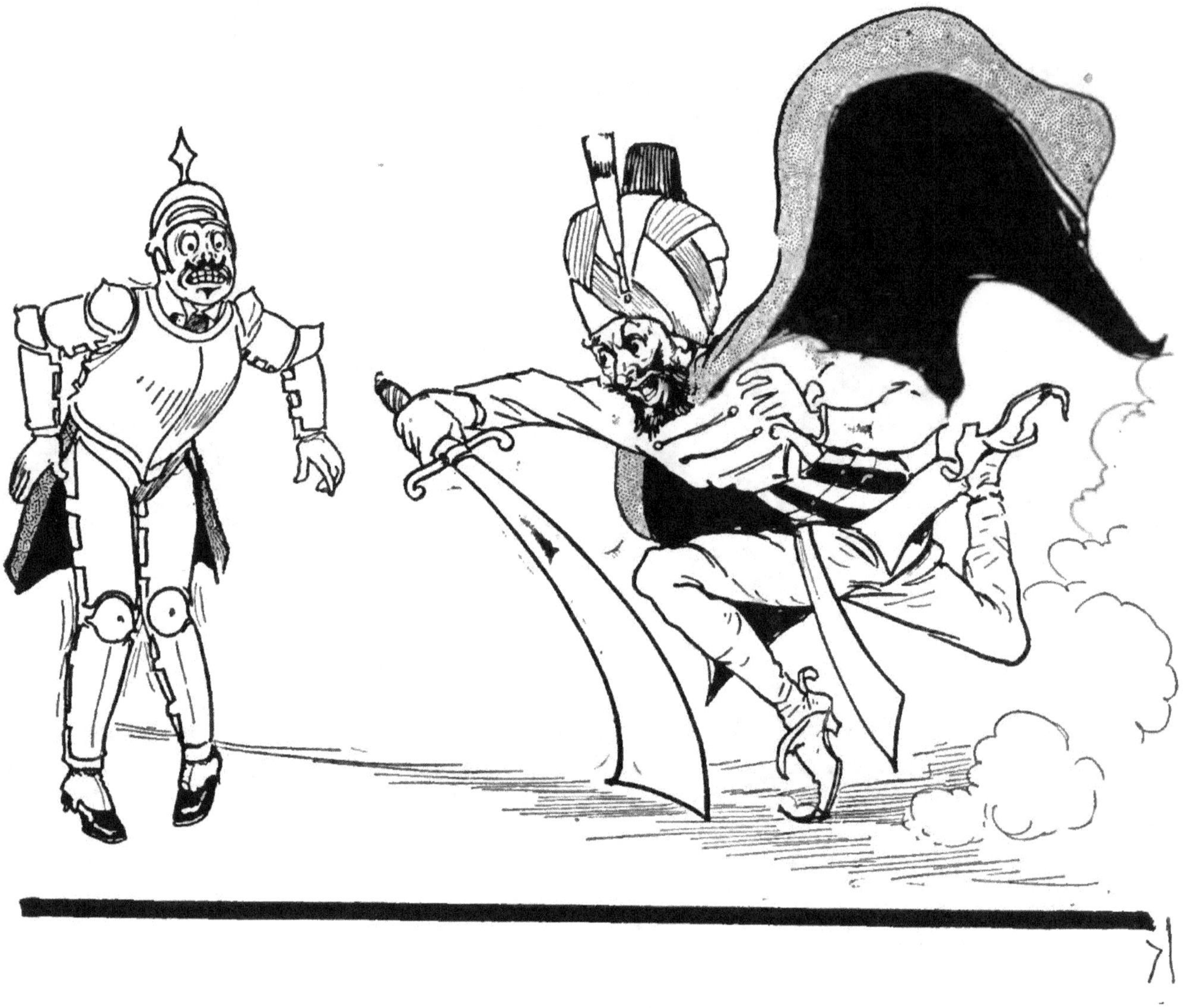

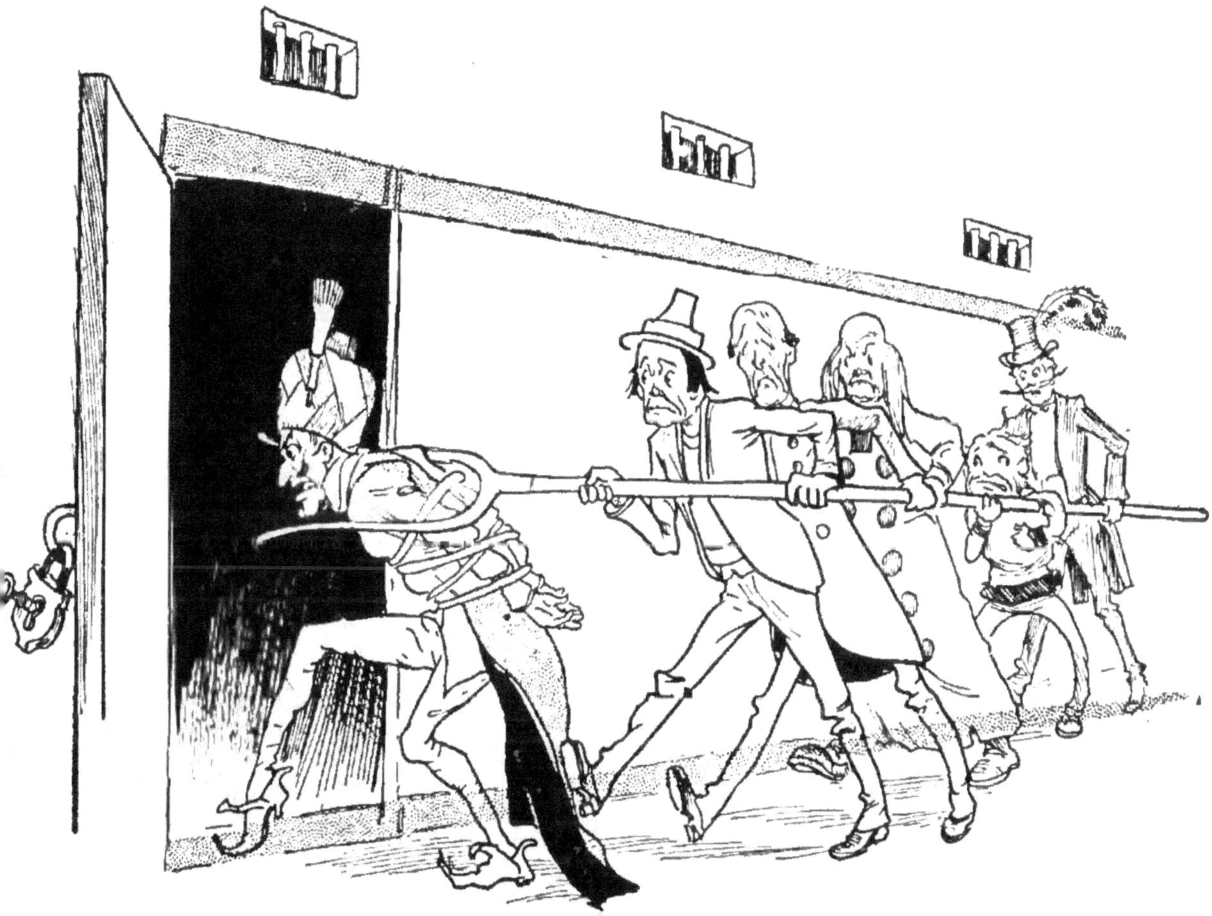

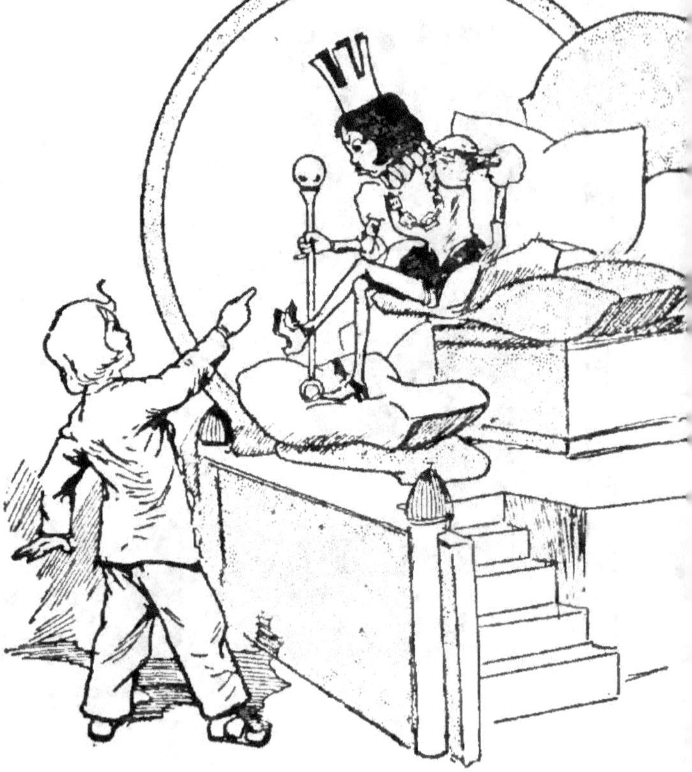

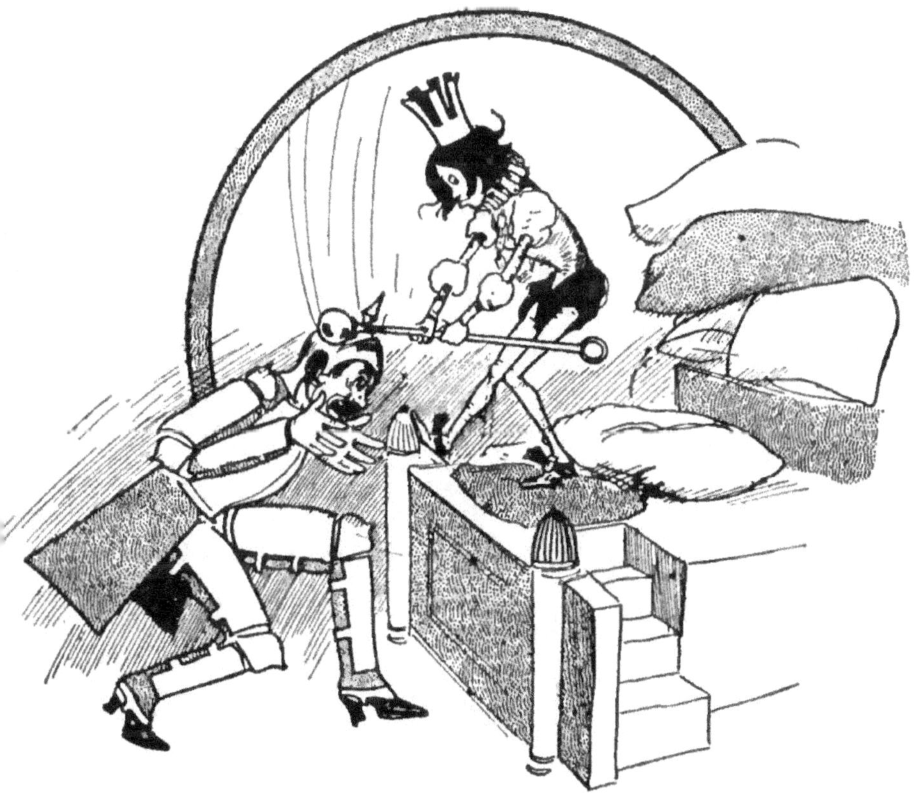

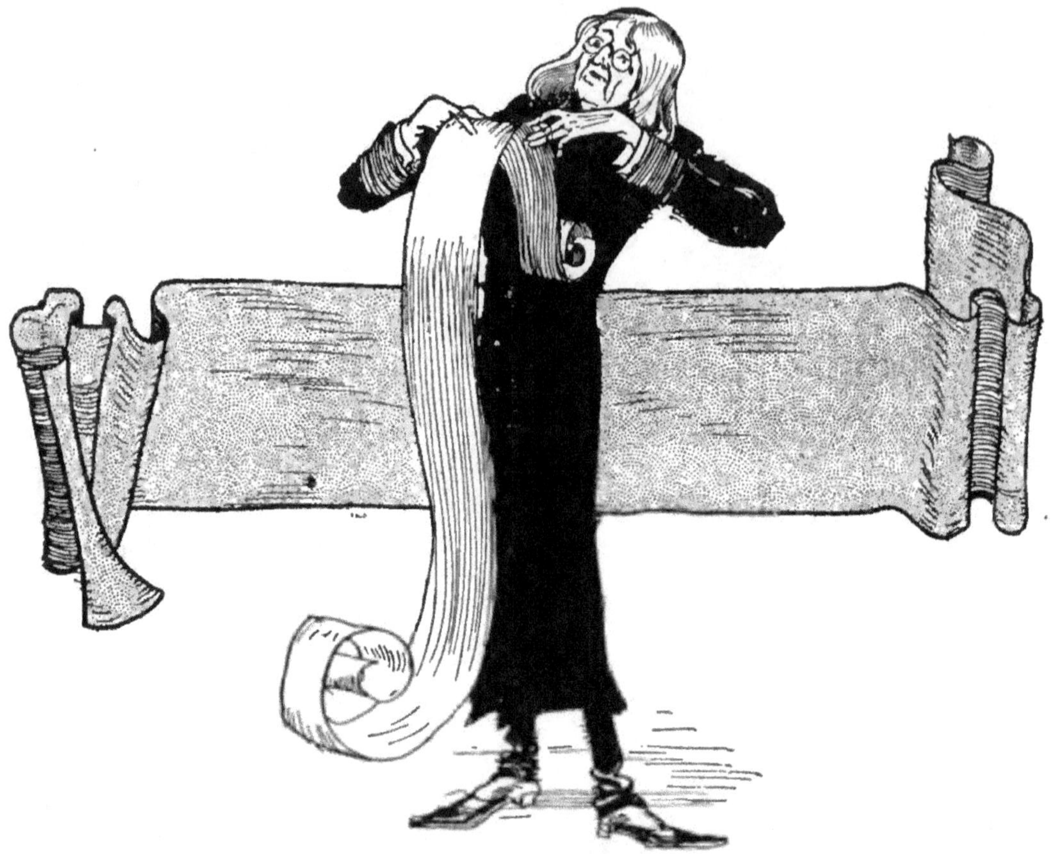

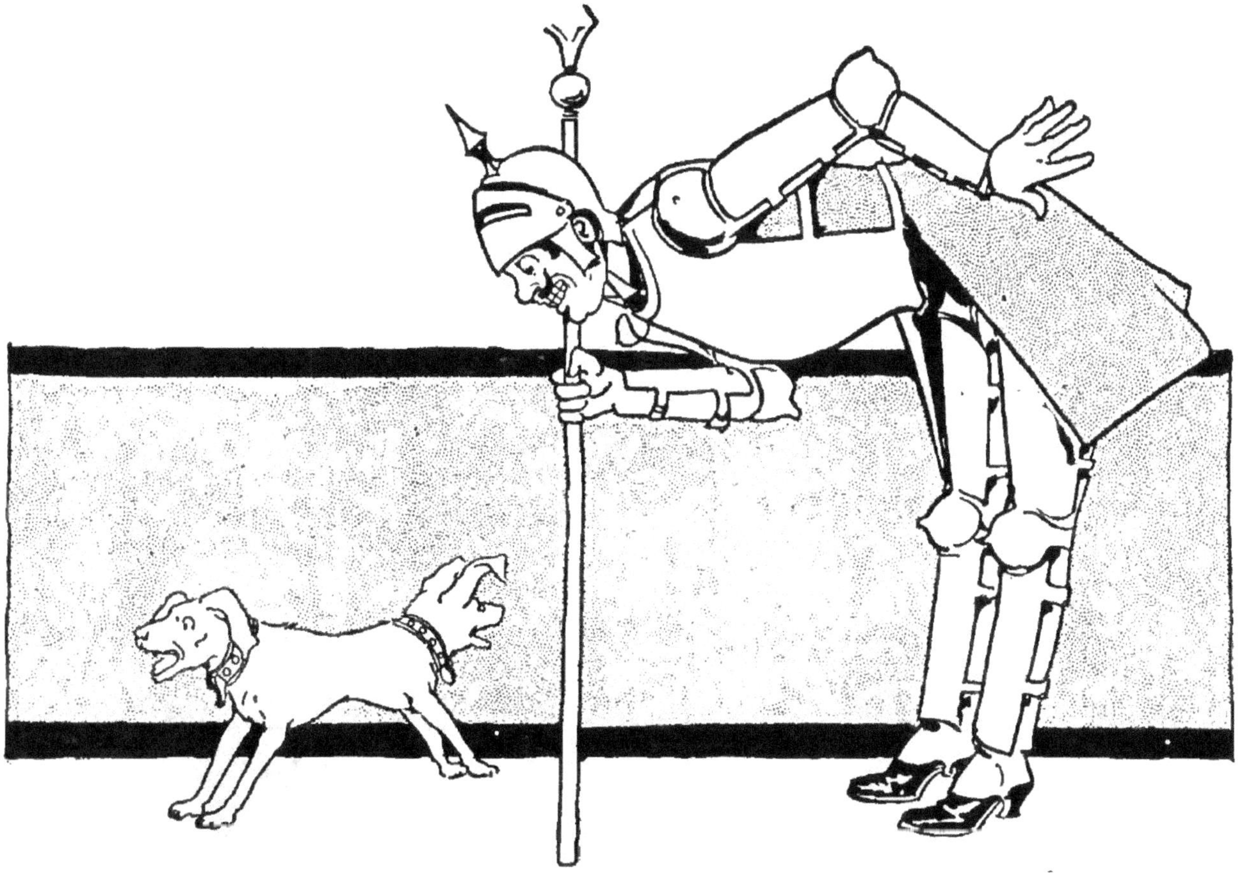

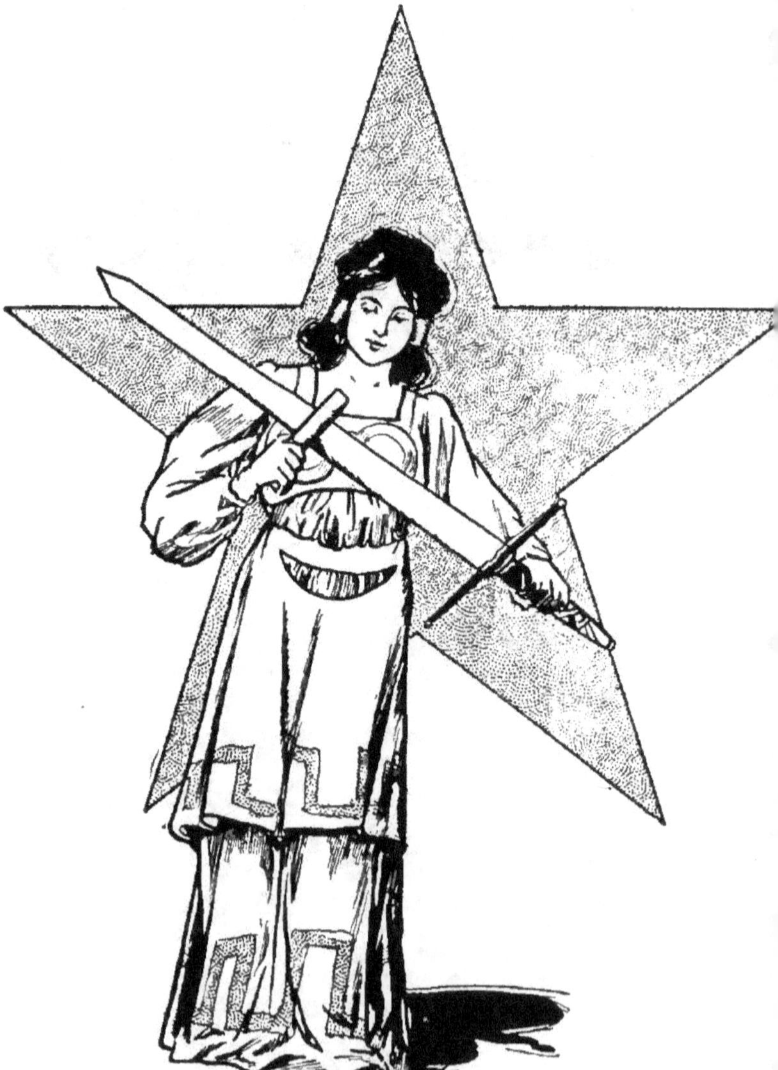

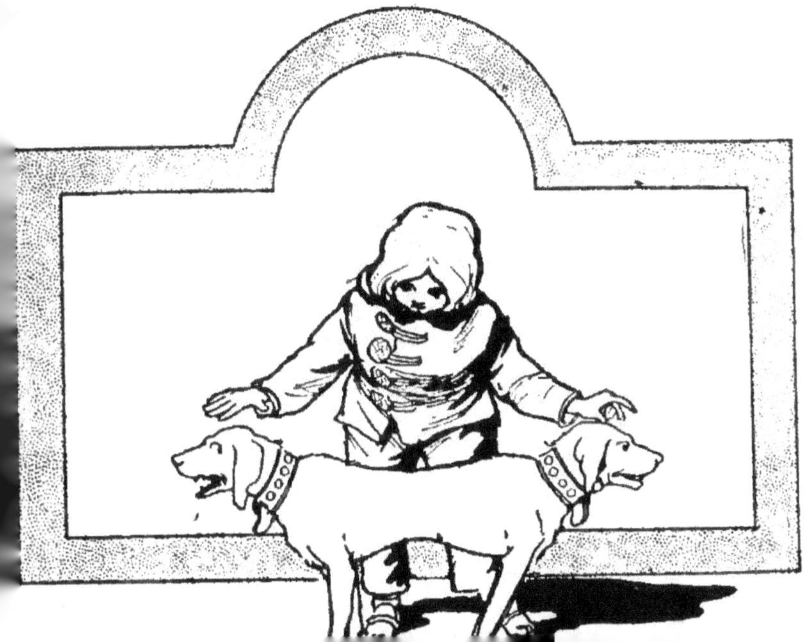

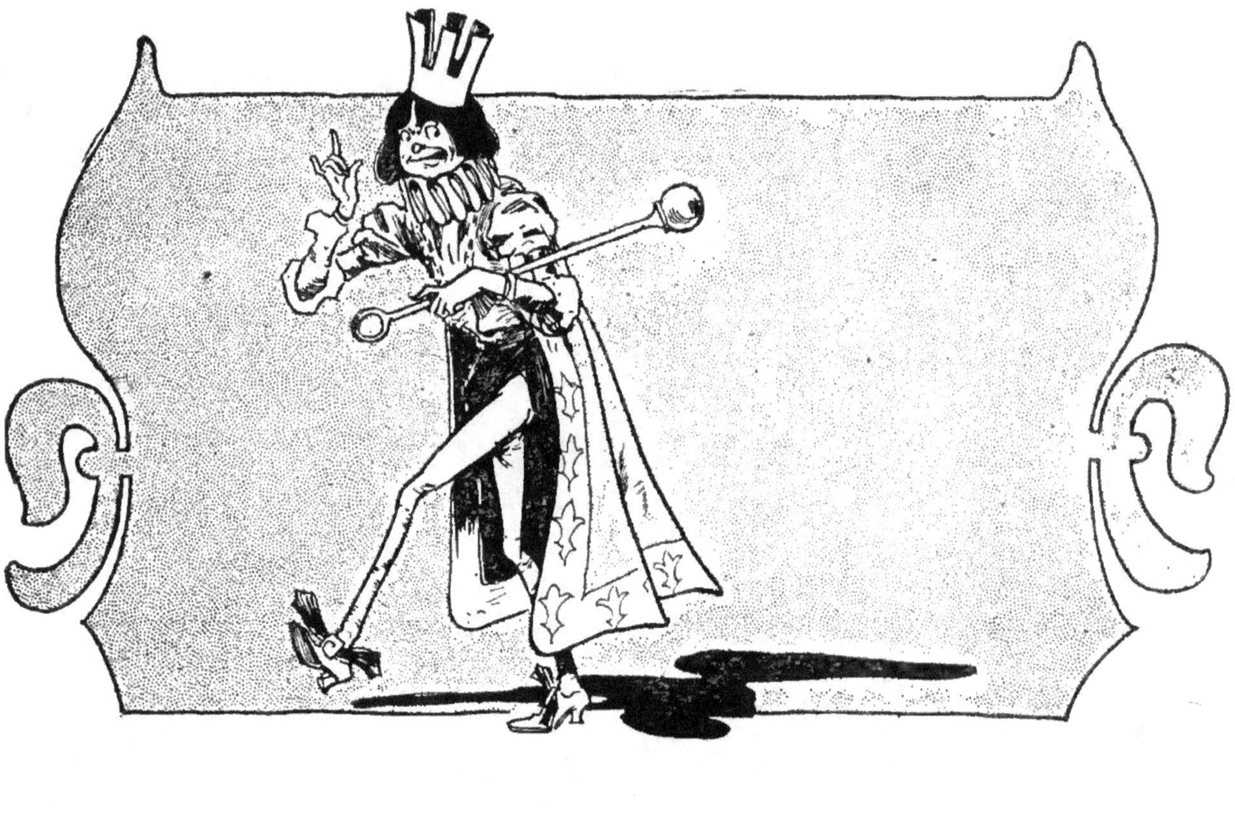

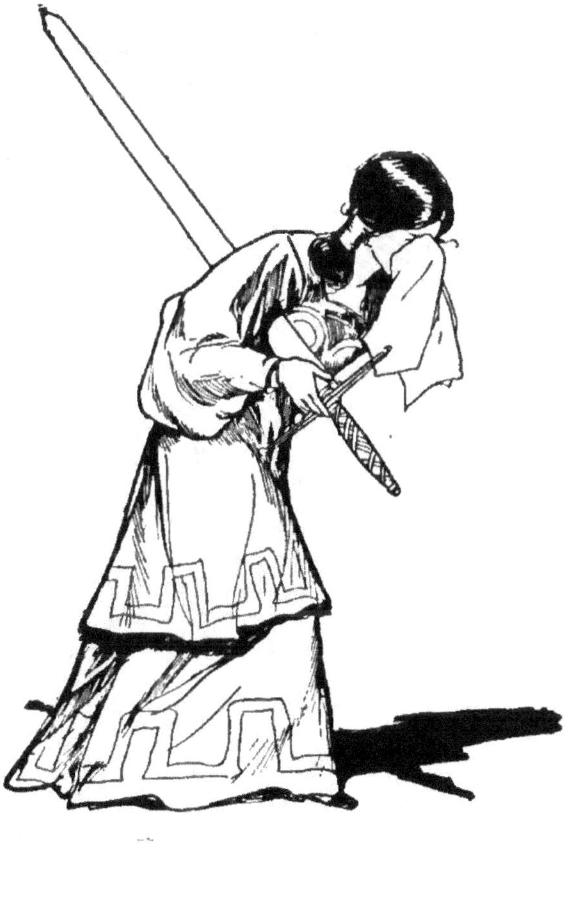

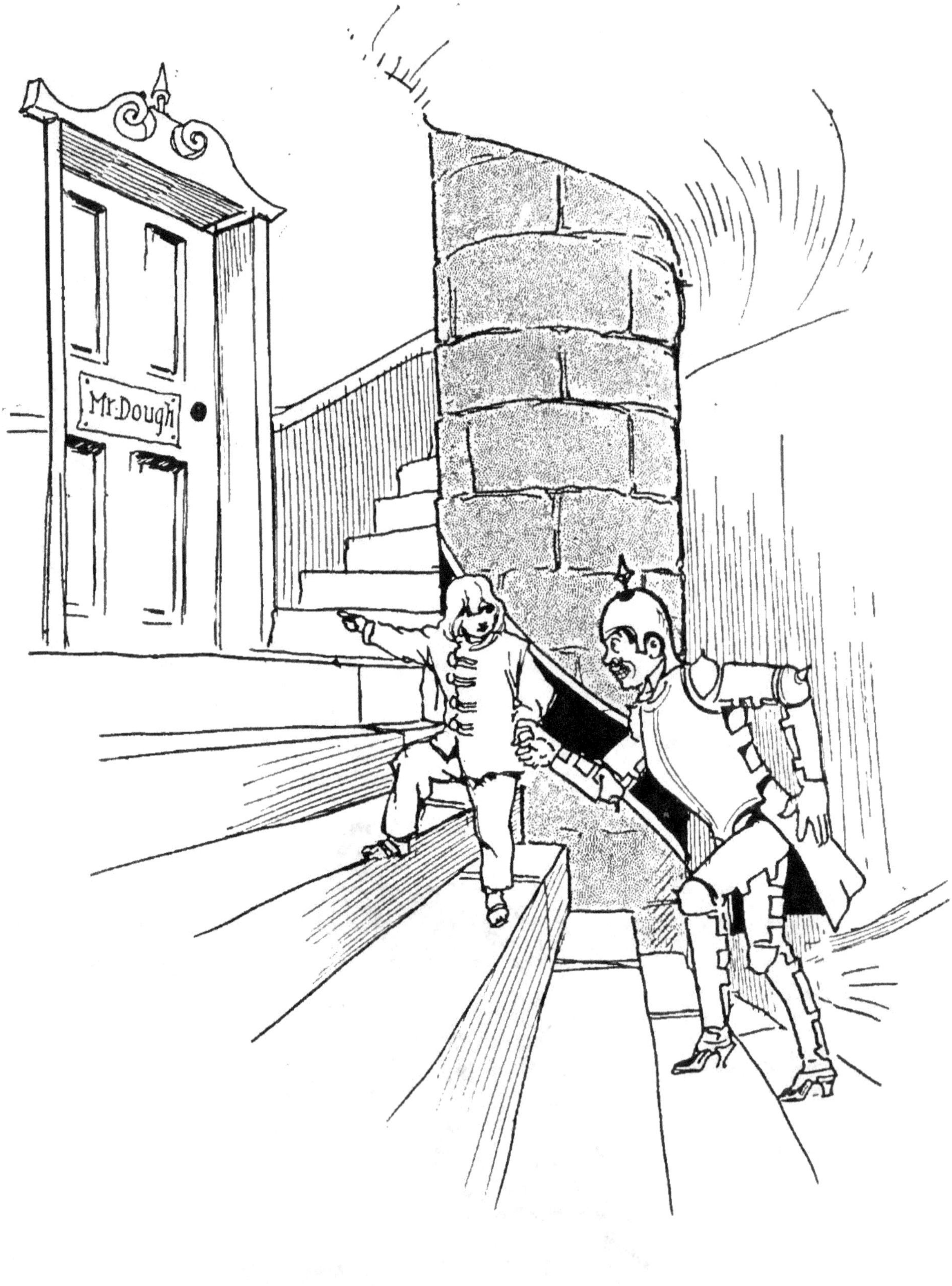
Mr Dough

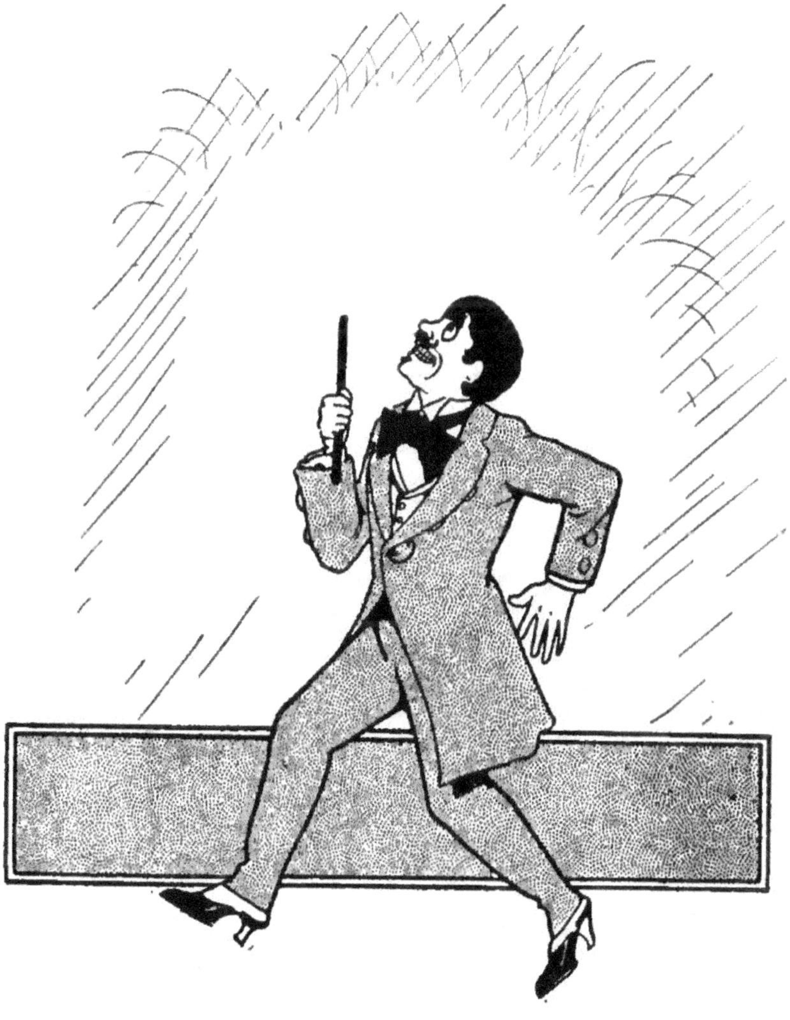

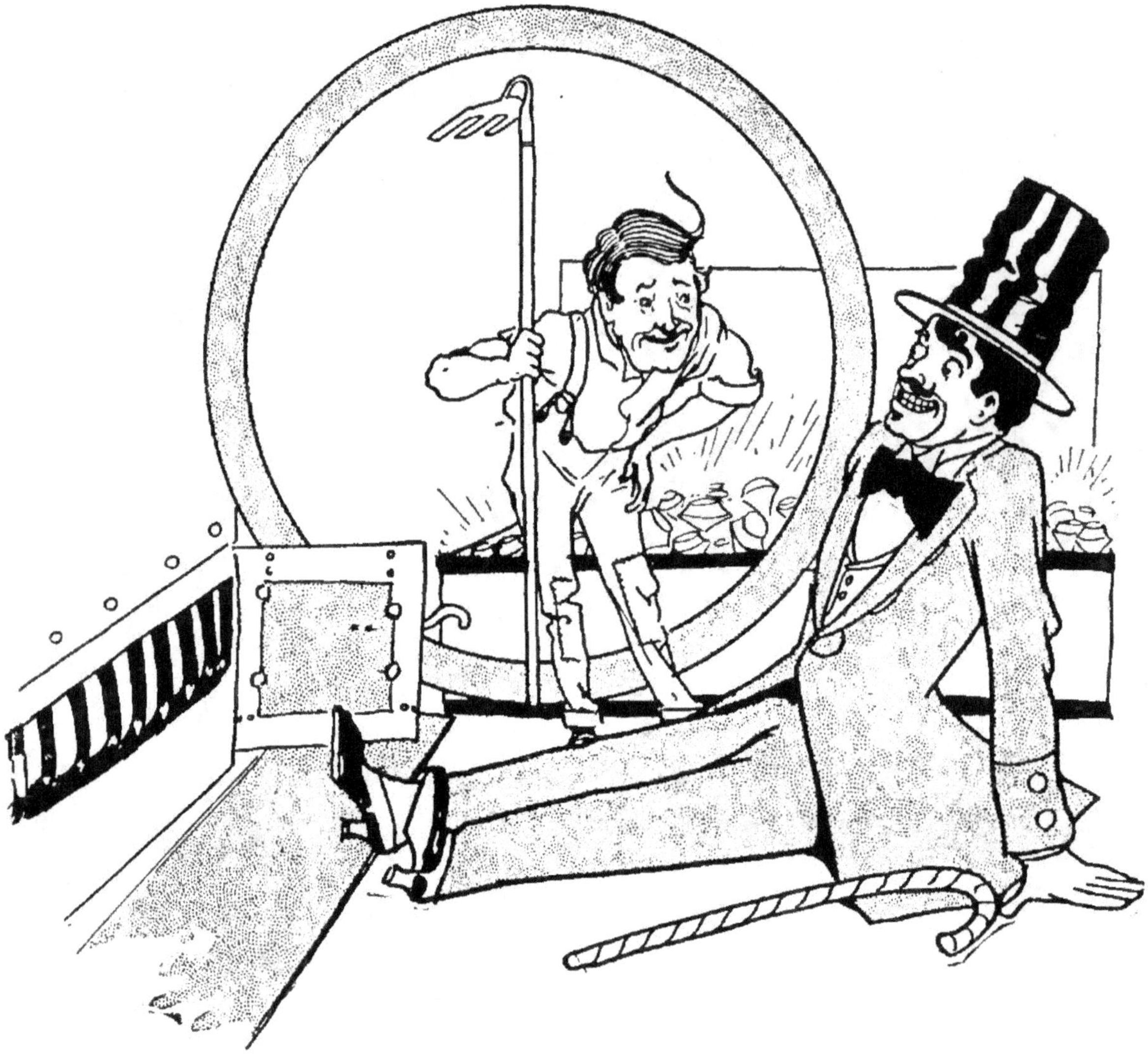

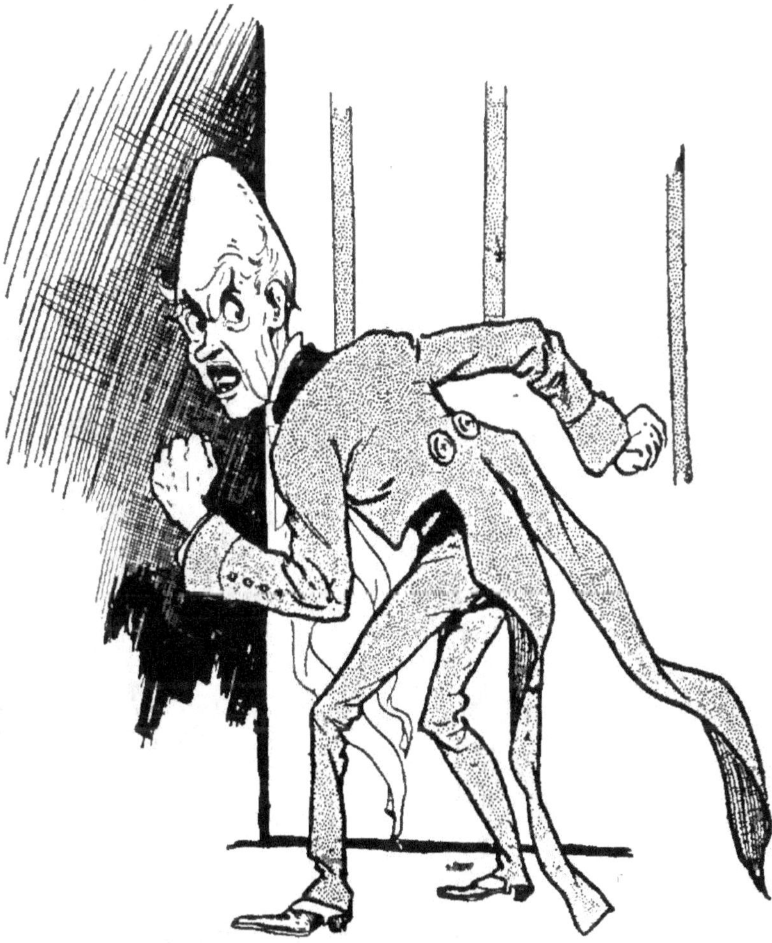

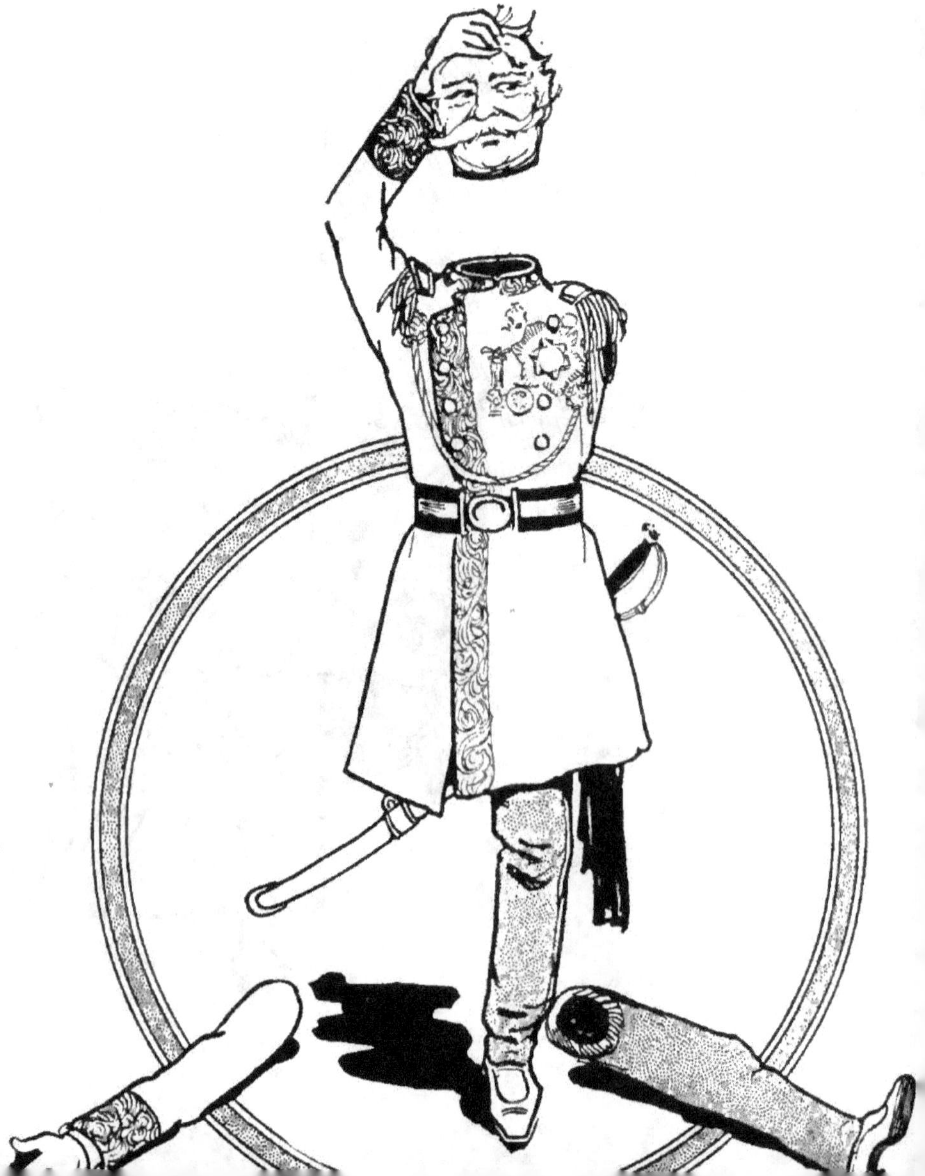

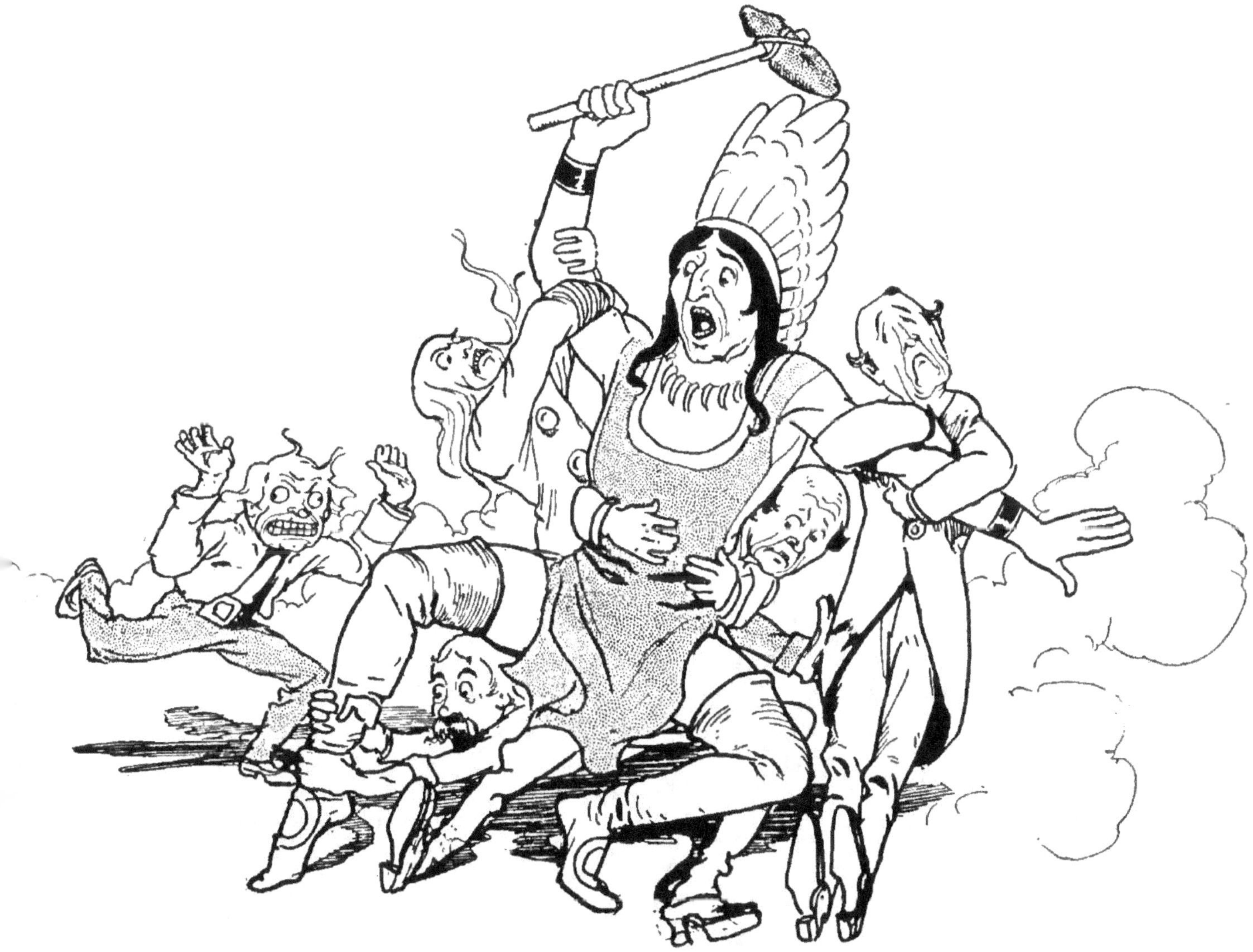

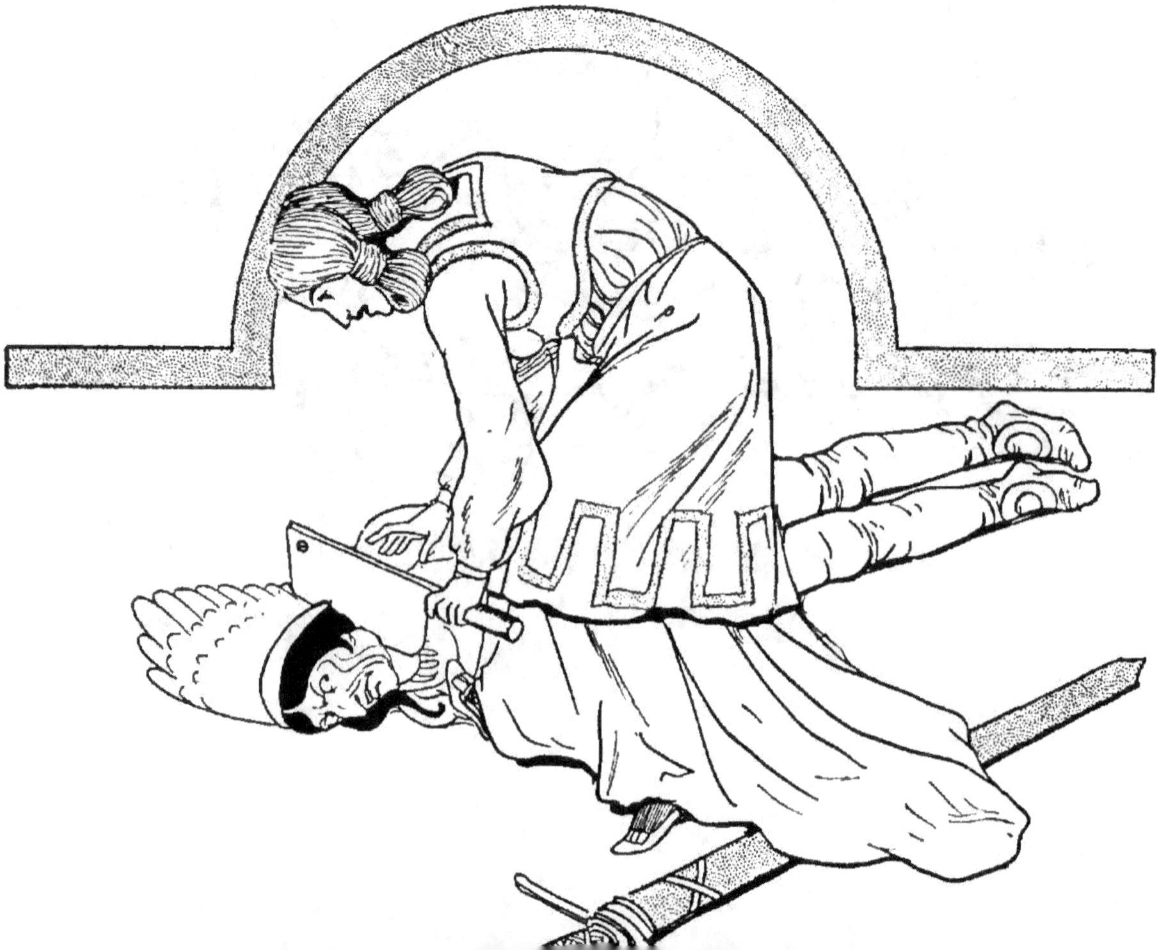

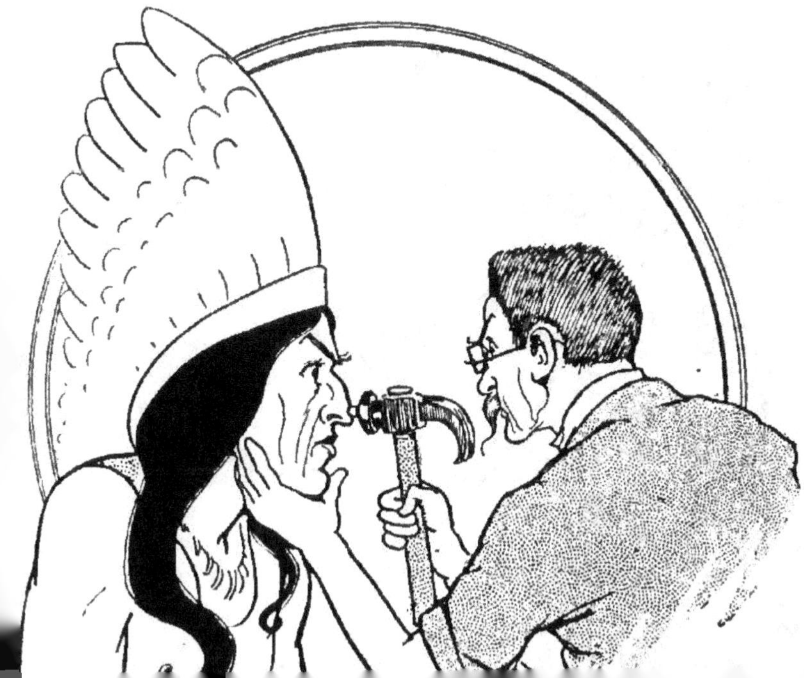

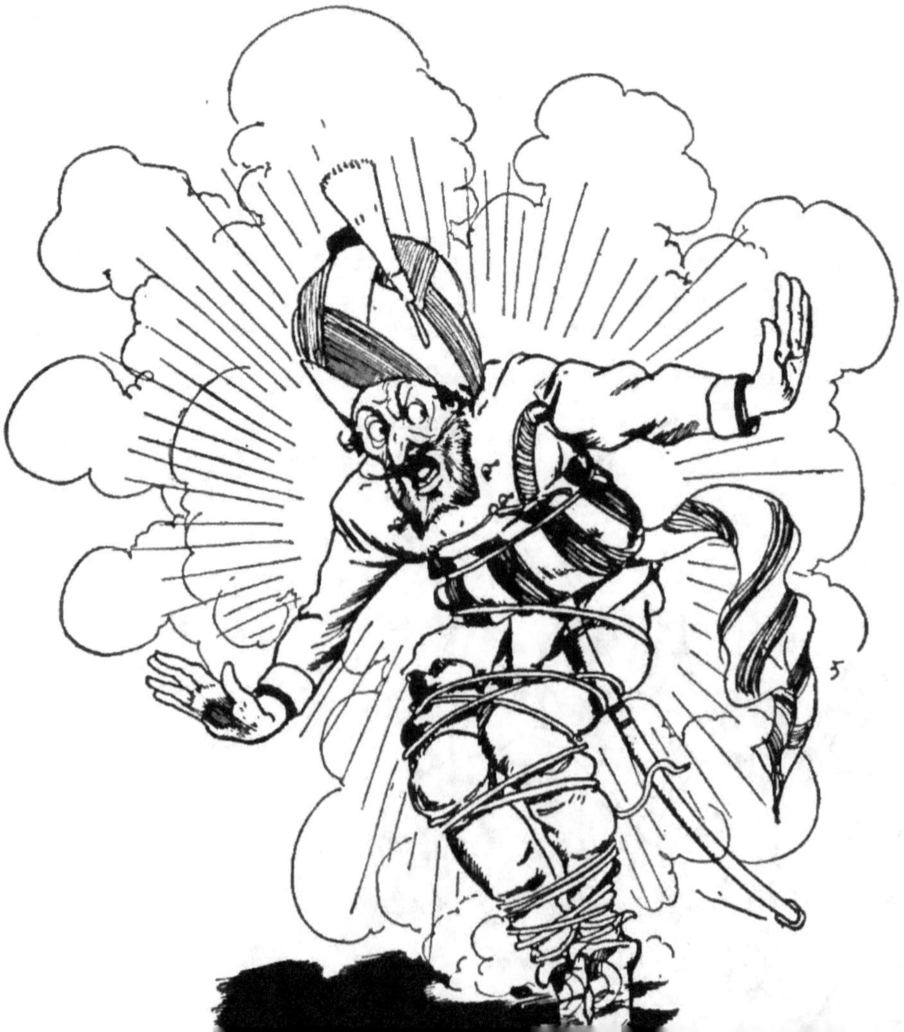

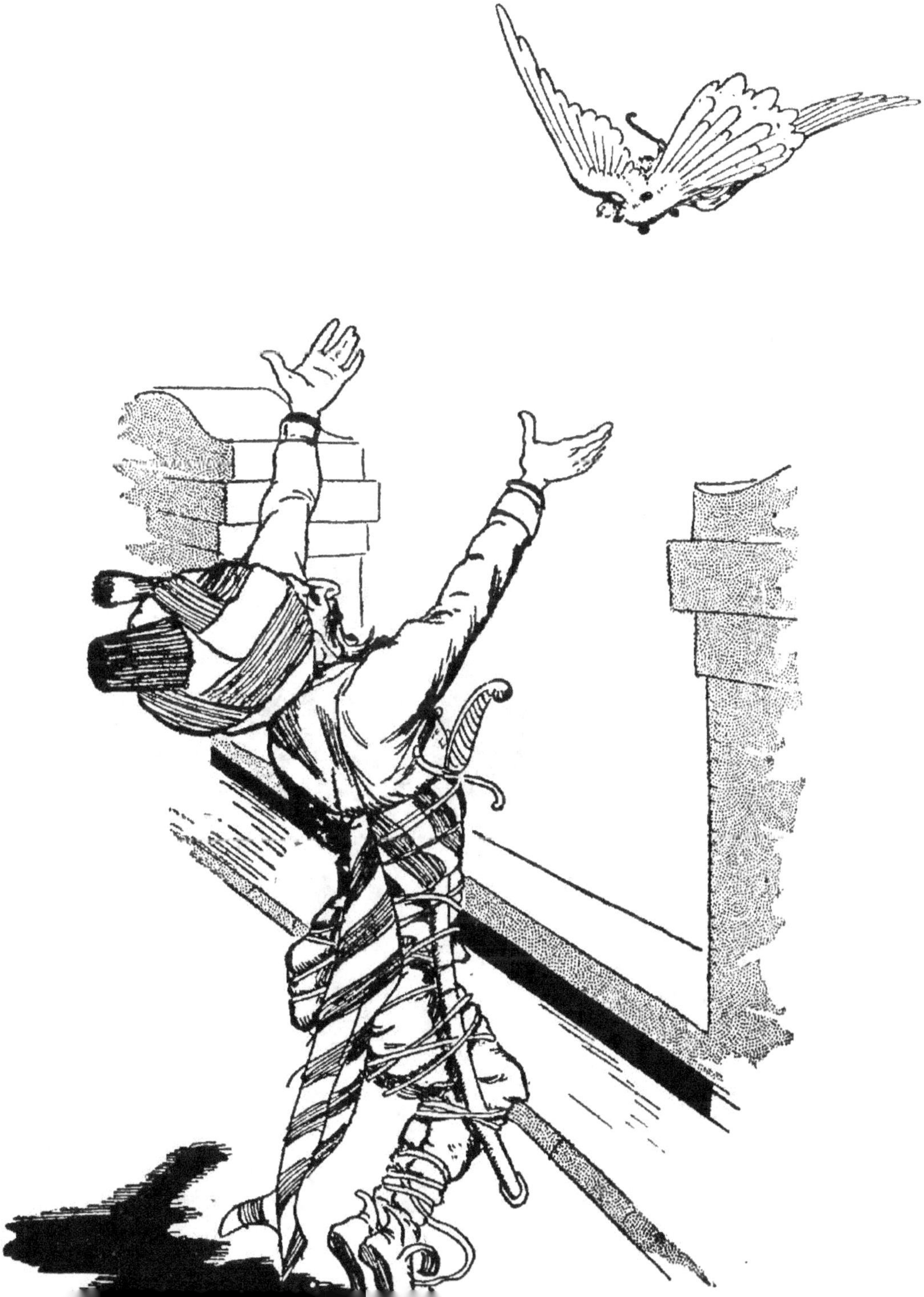

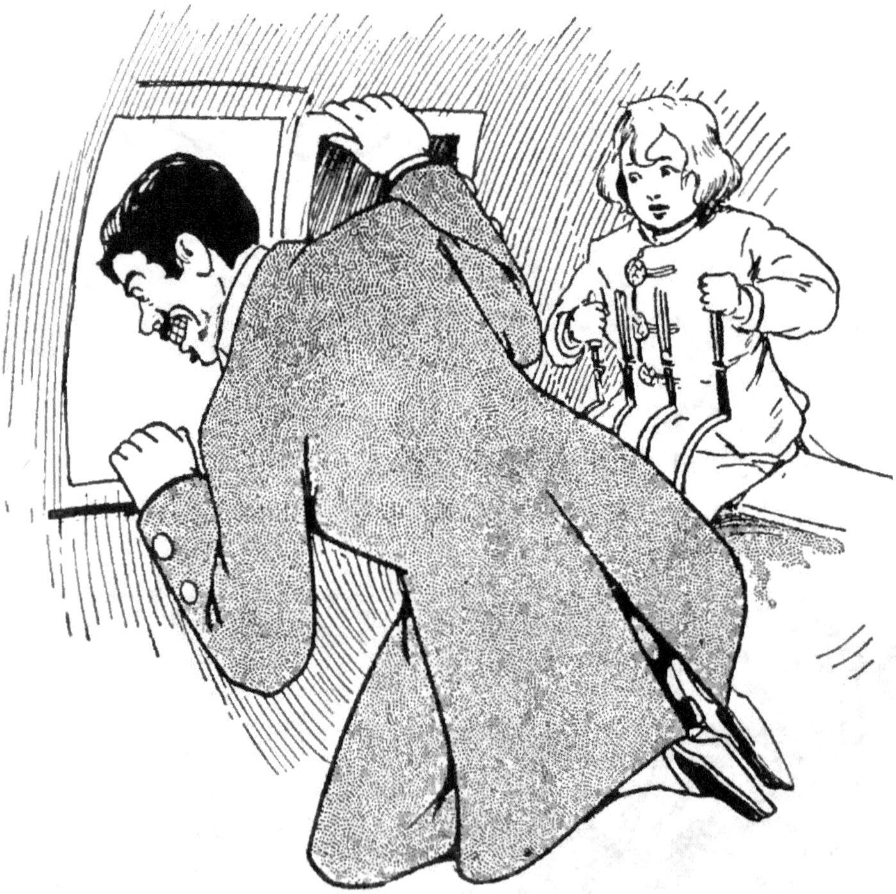

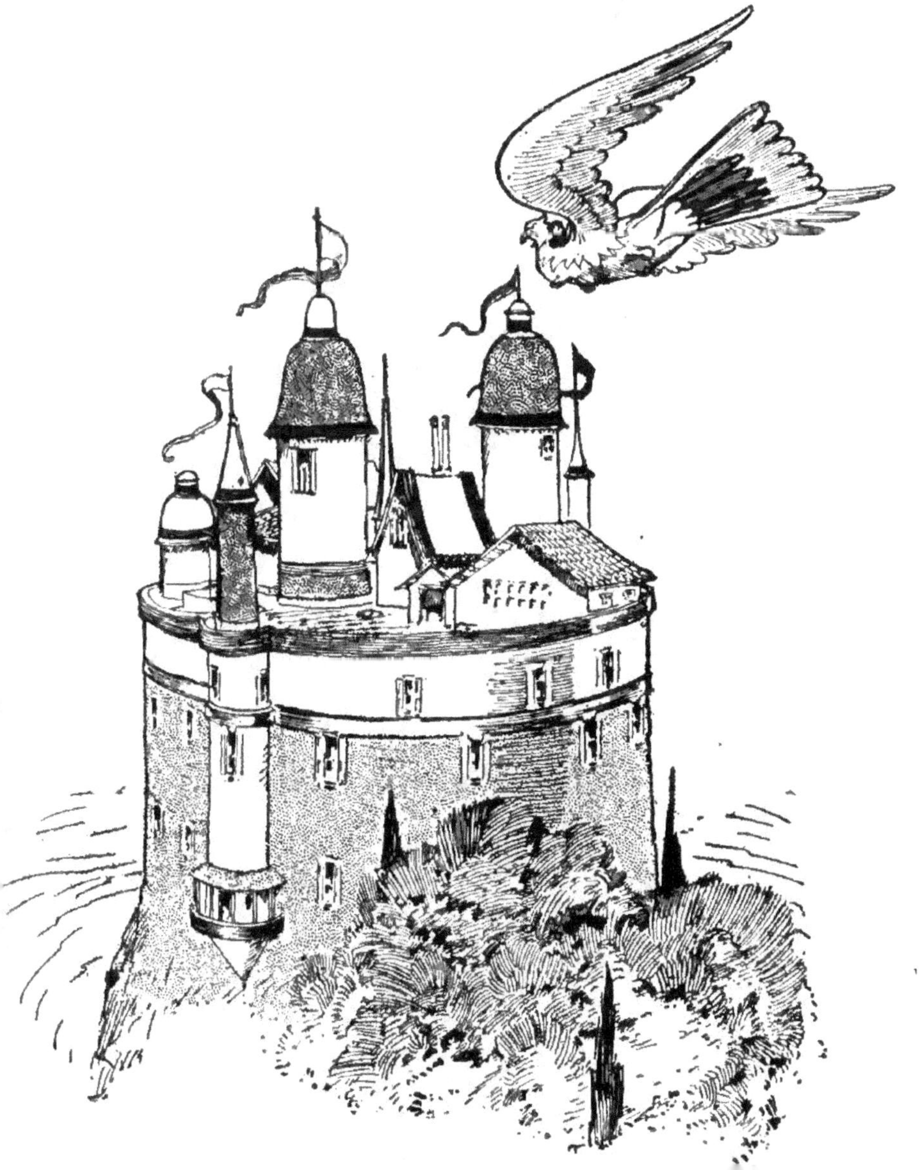

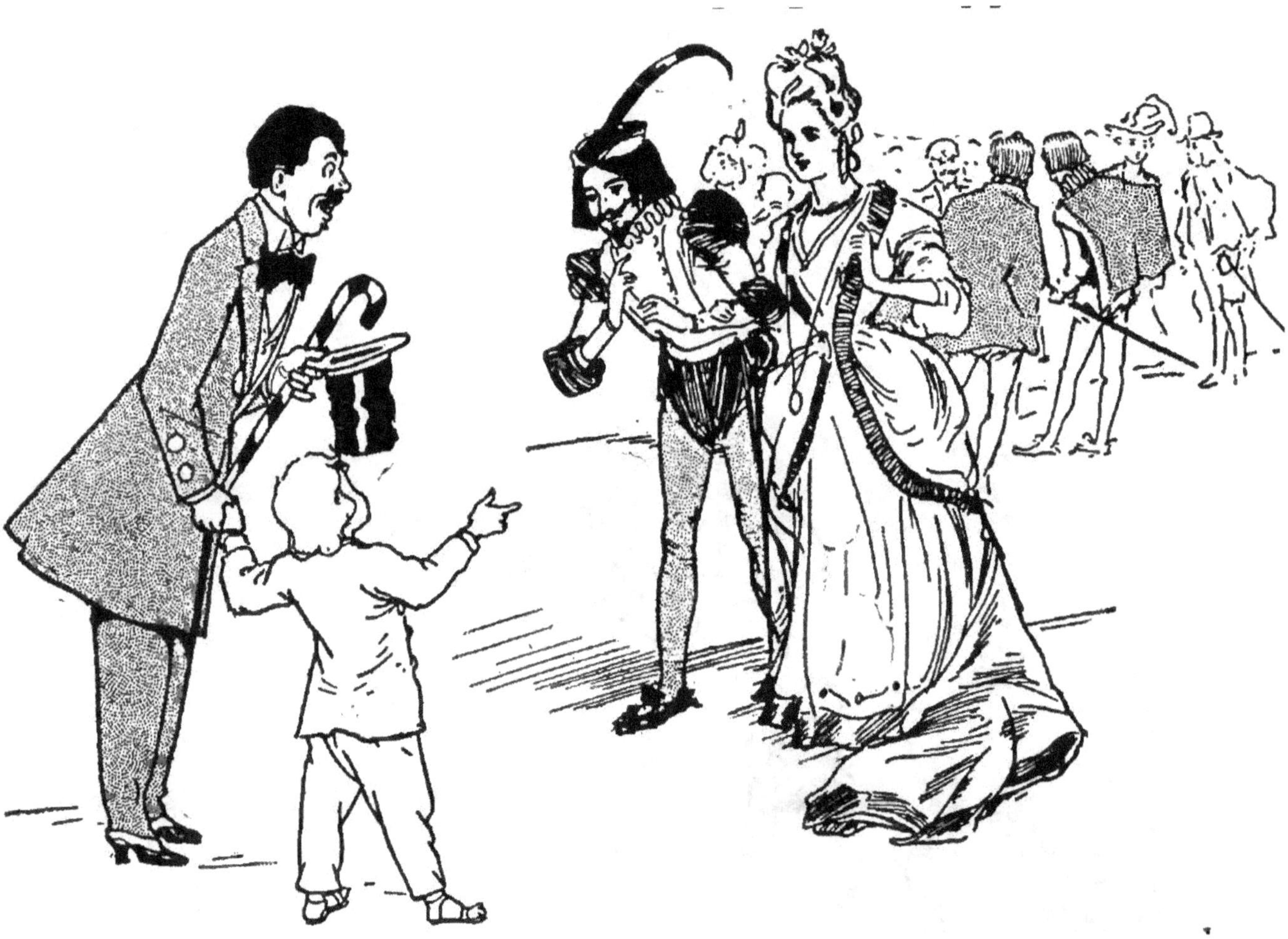

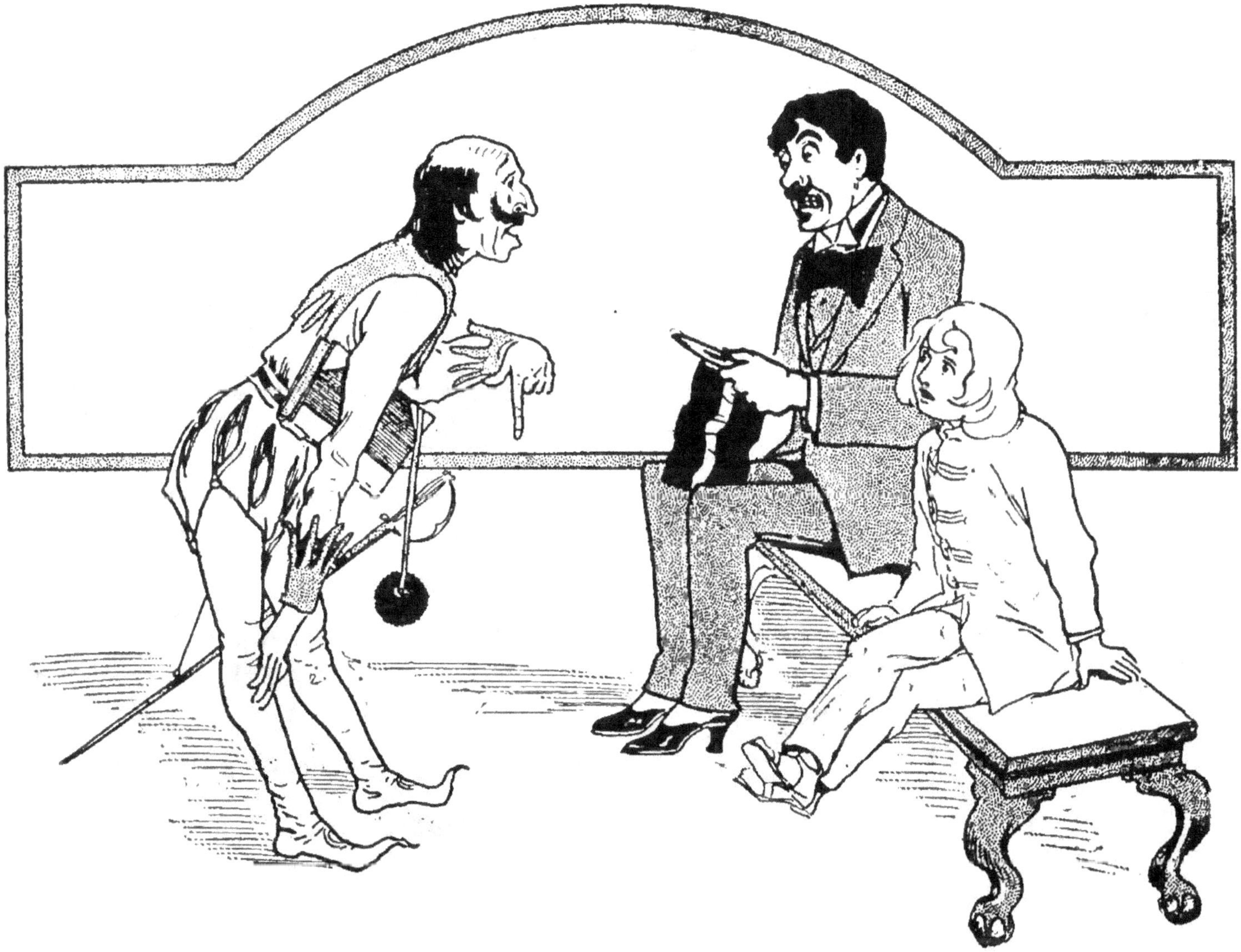

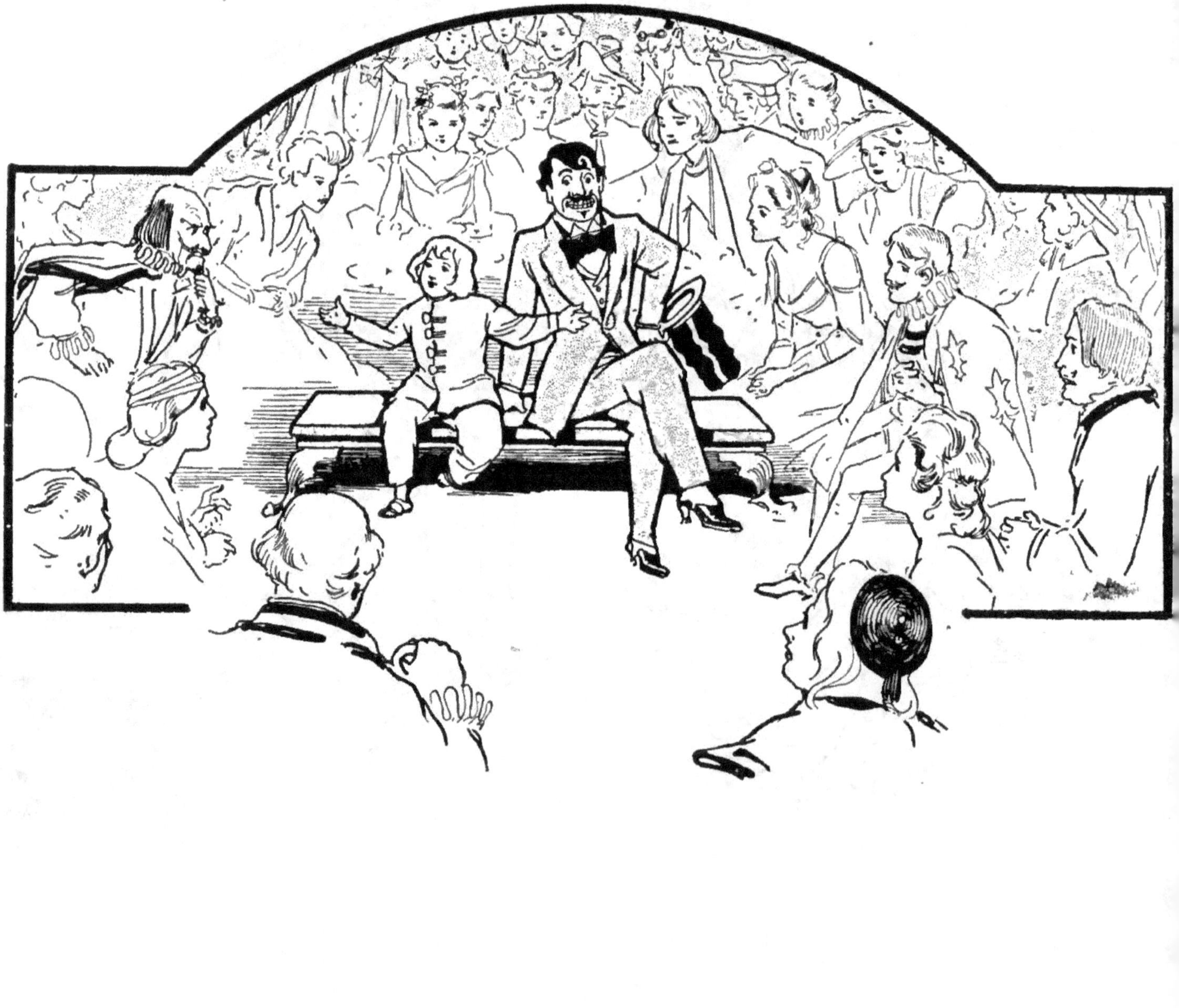

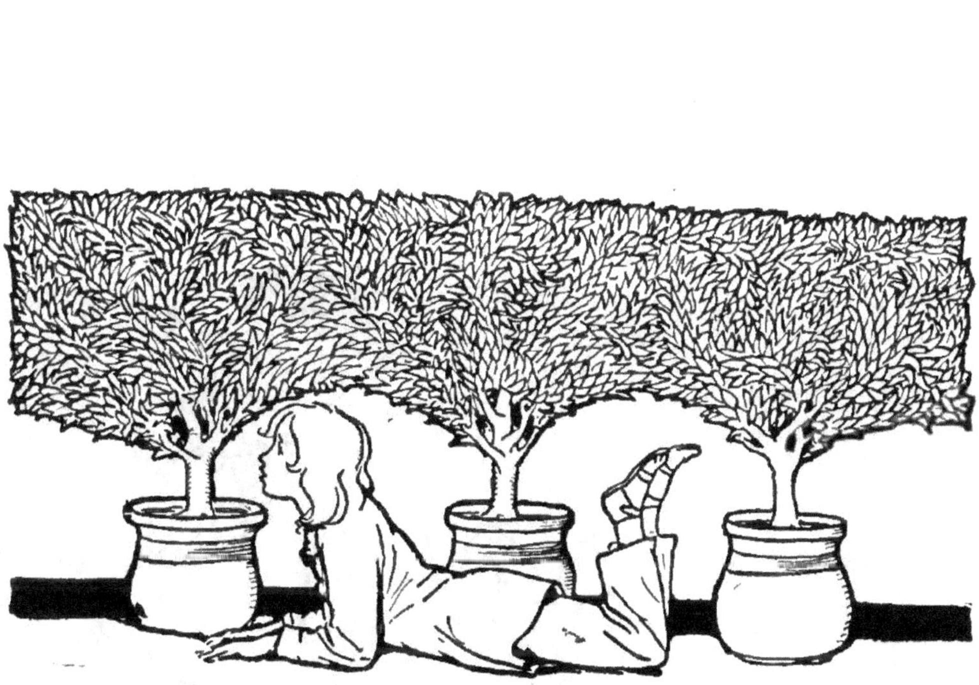

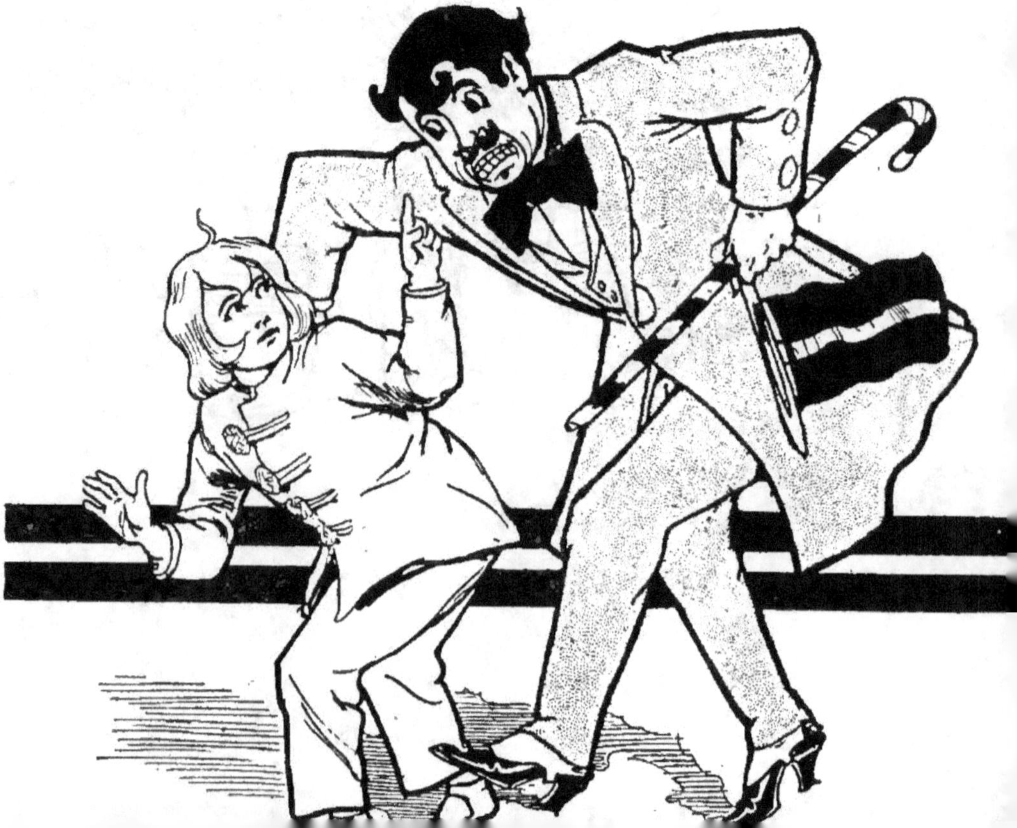

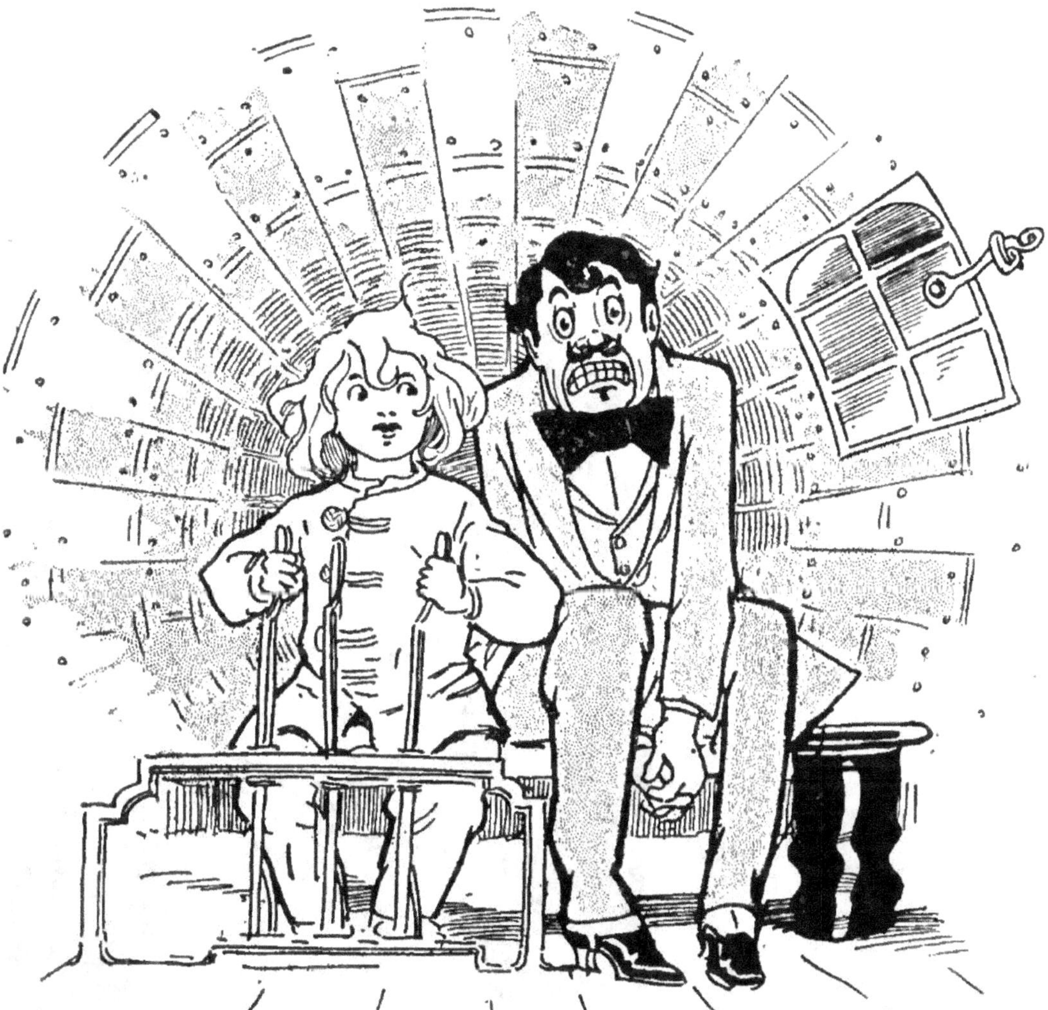

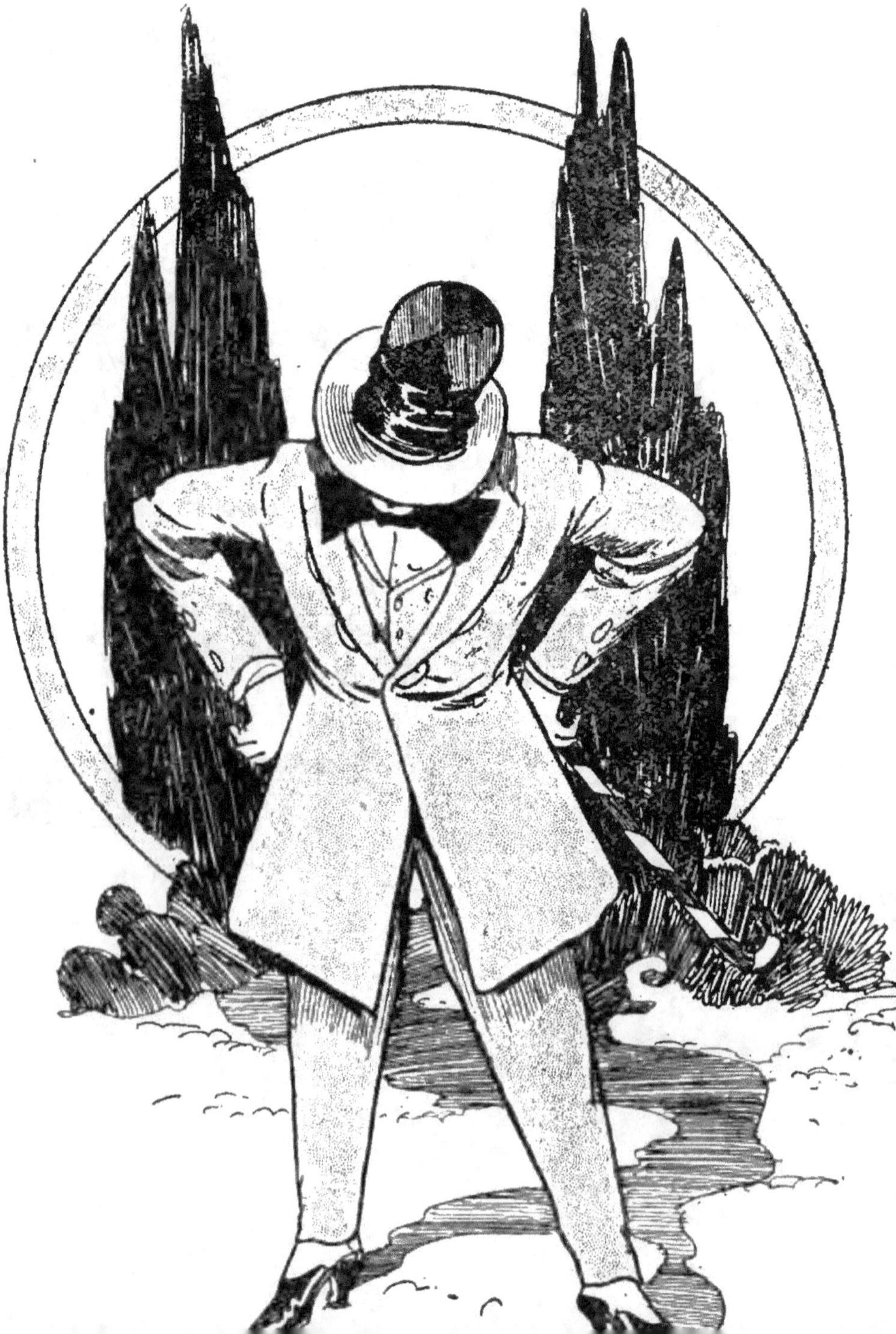

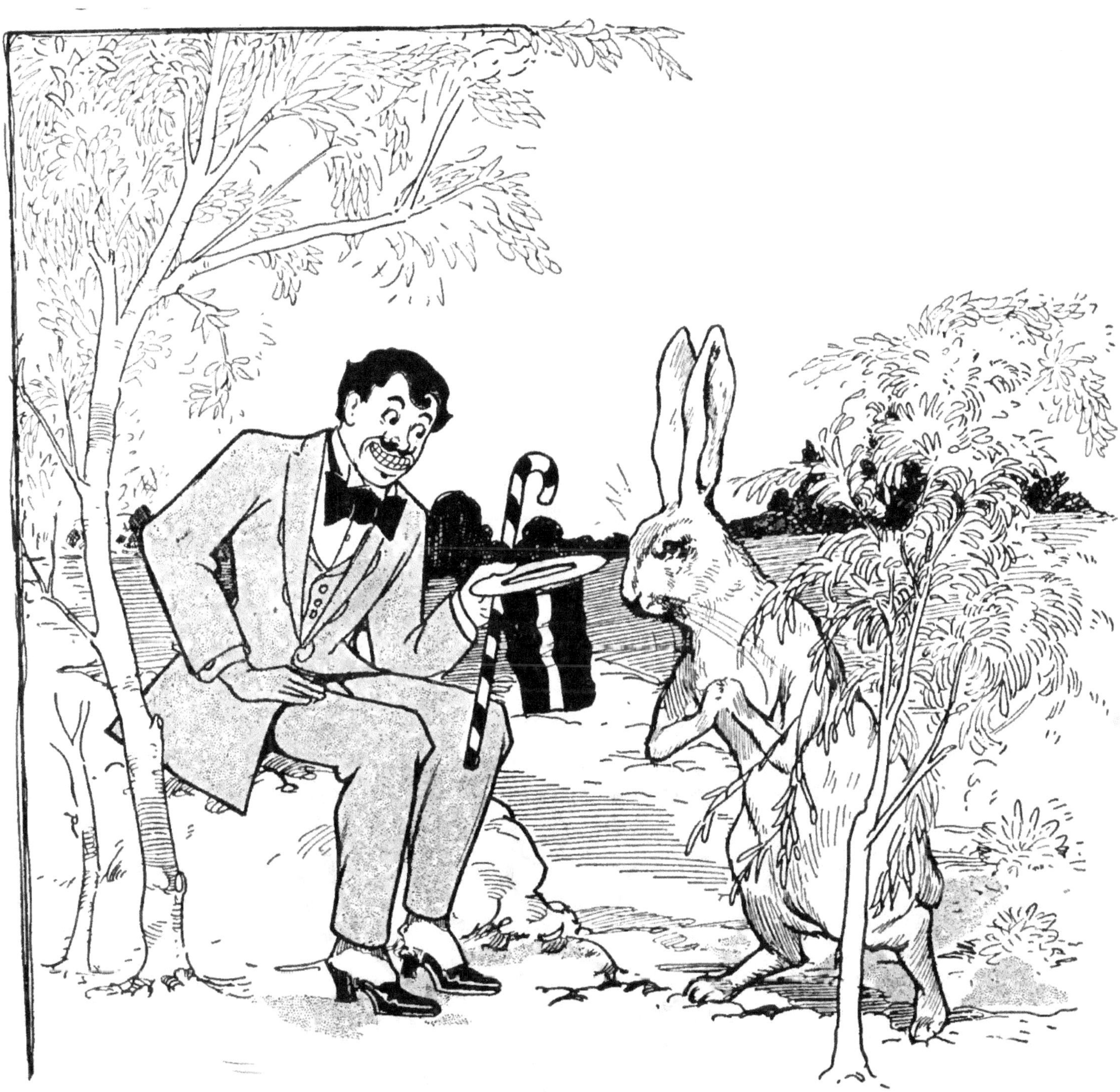

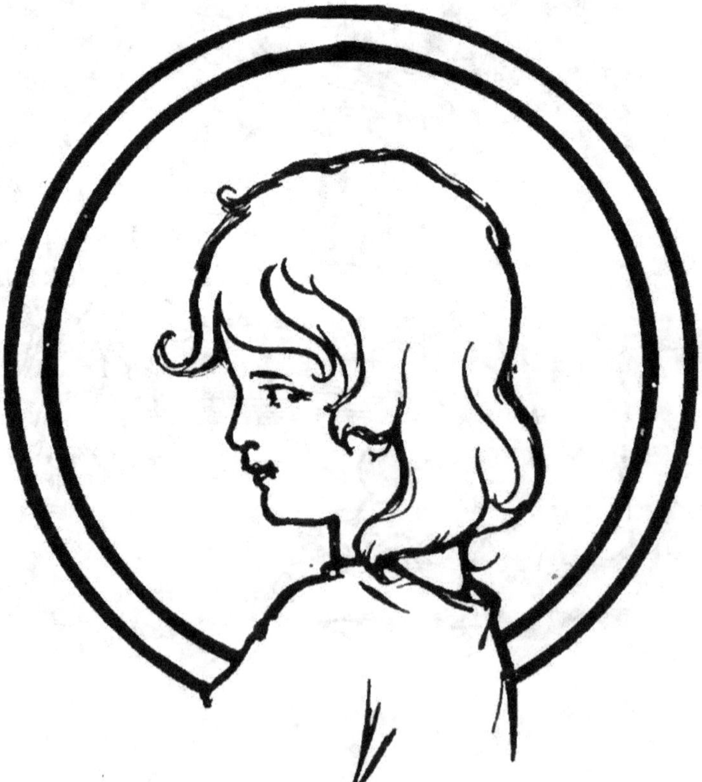

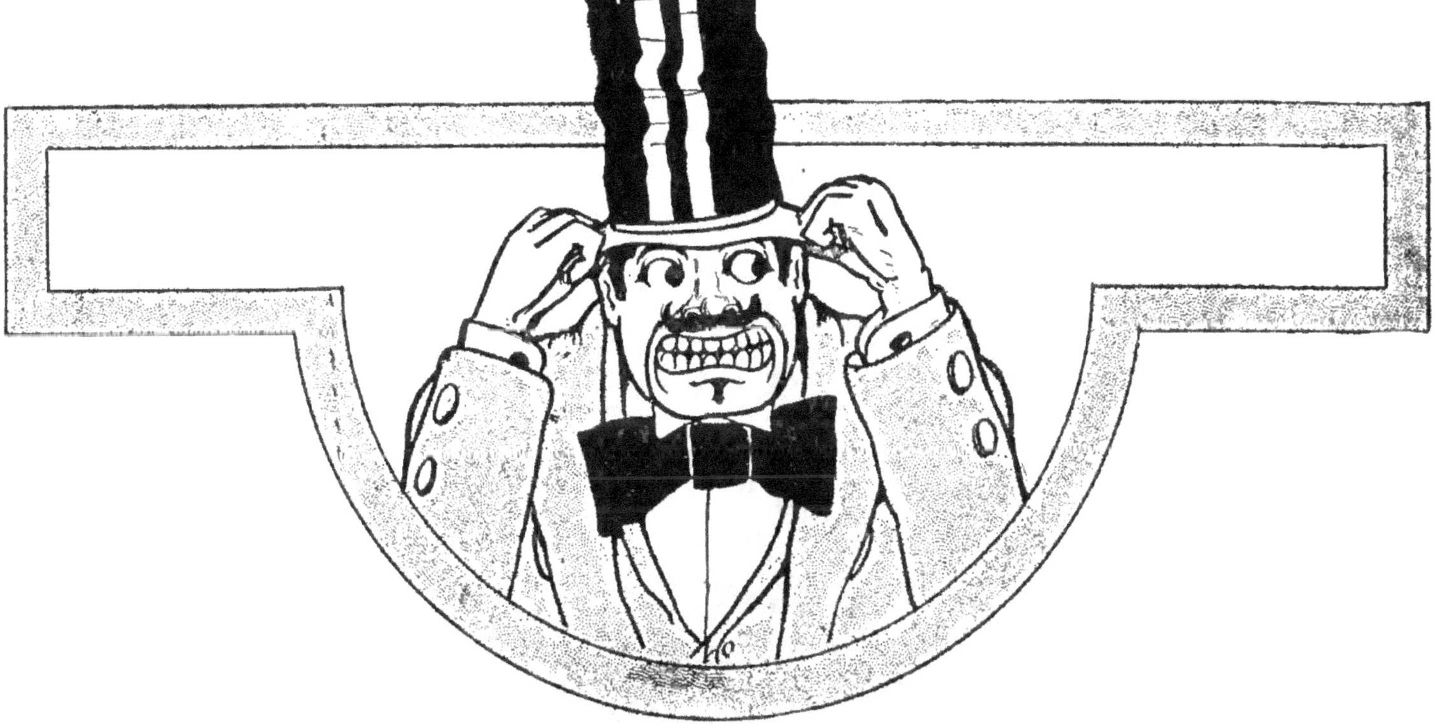

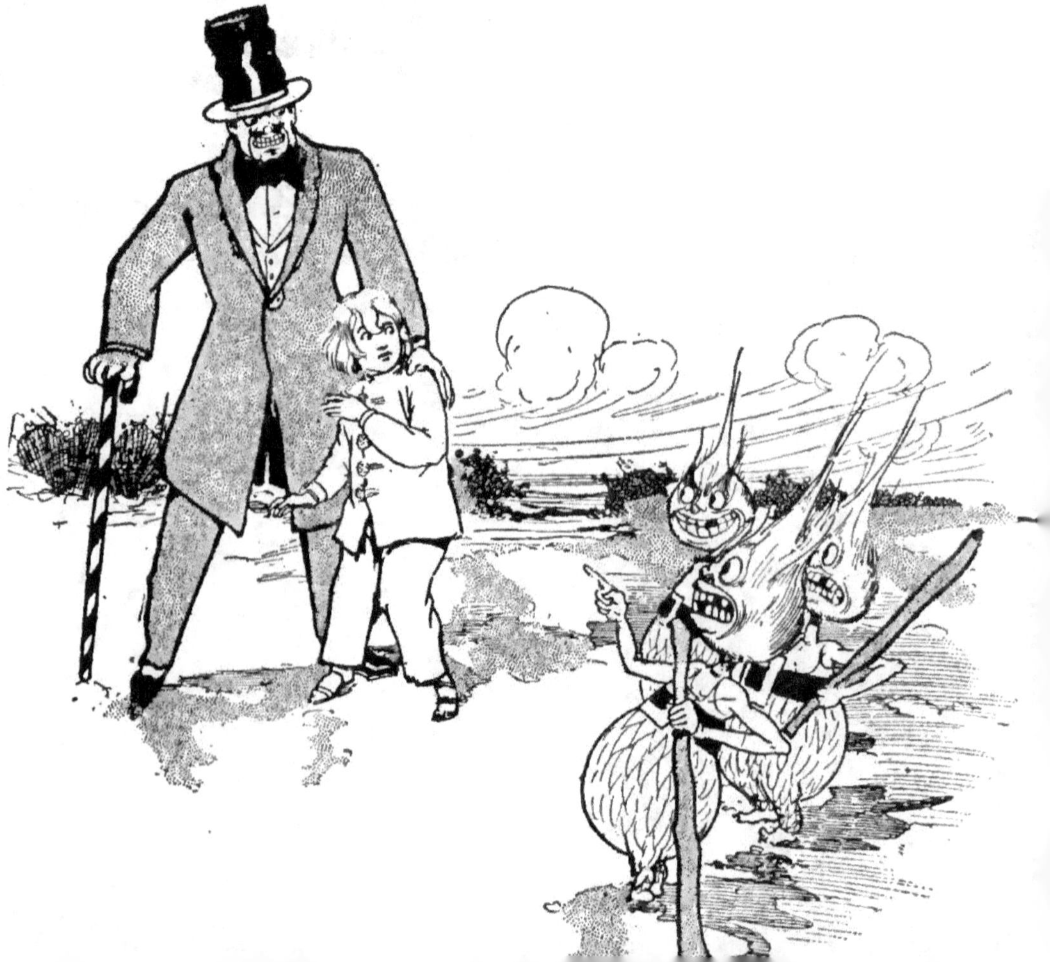

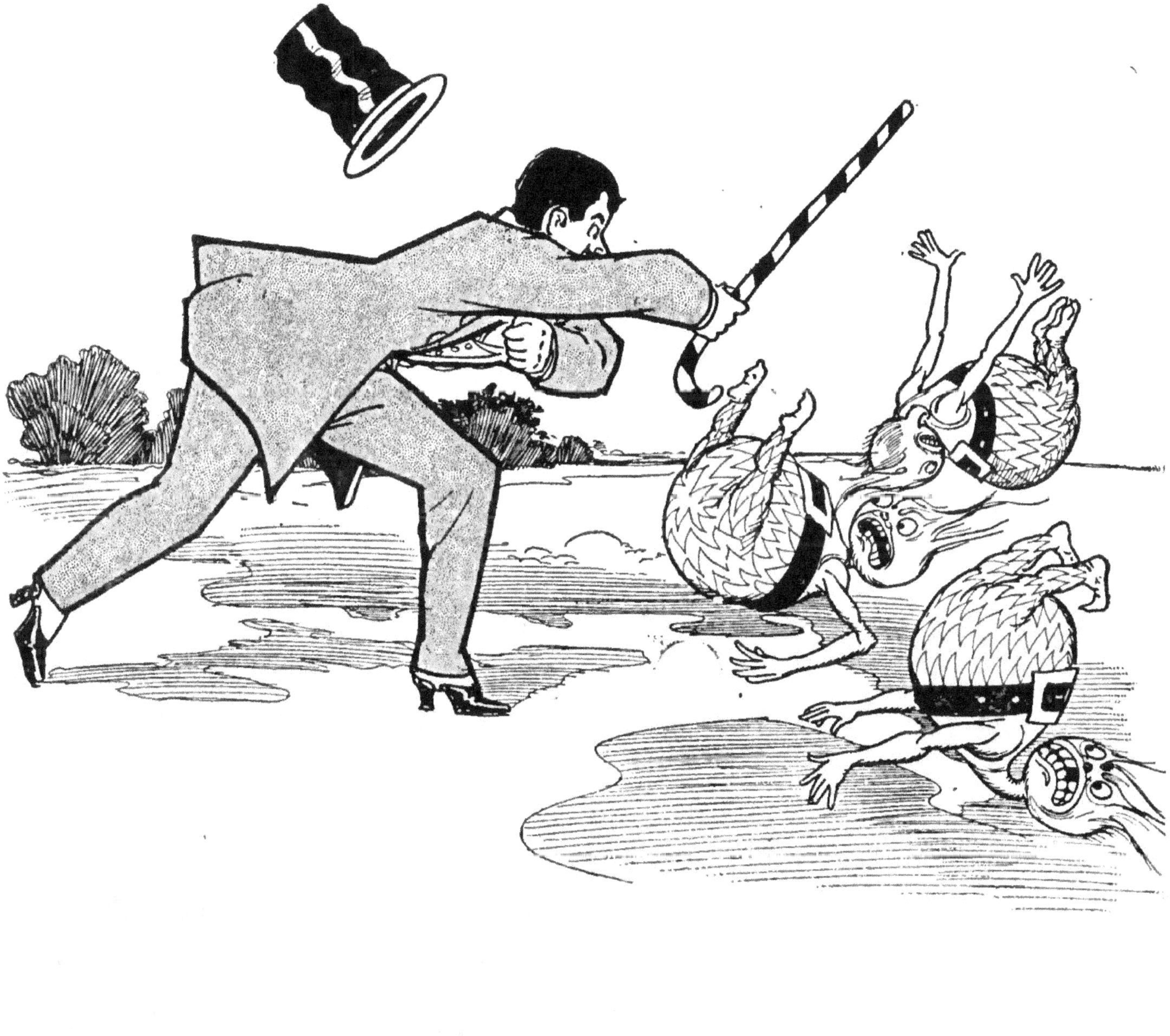

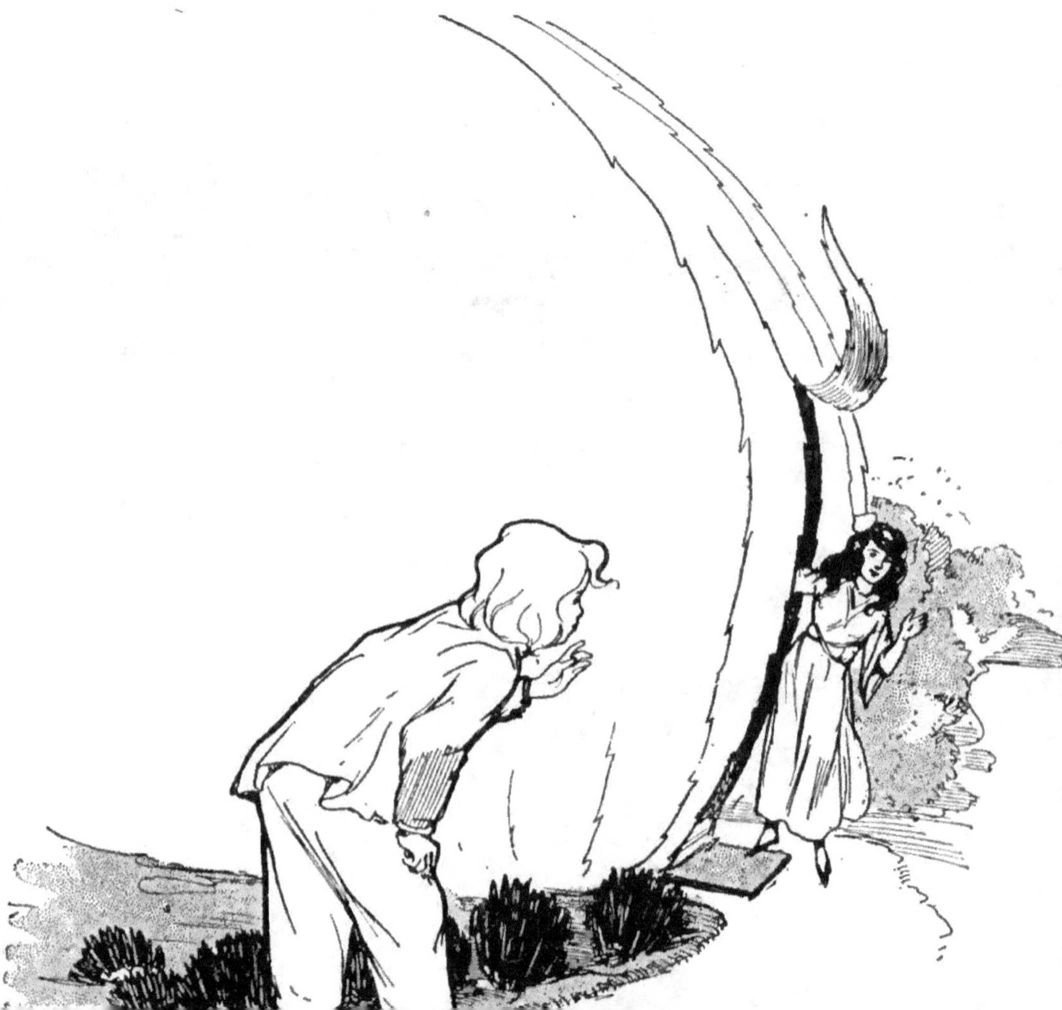

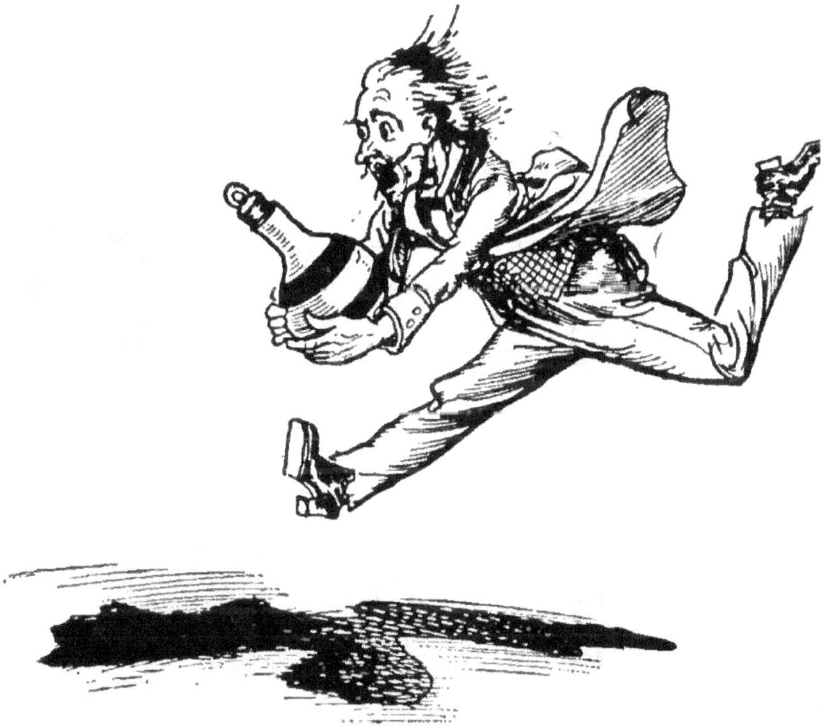

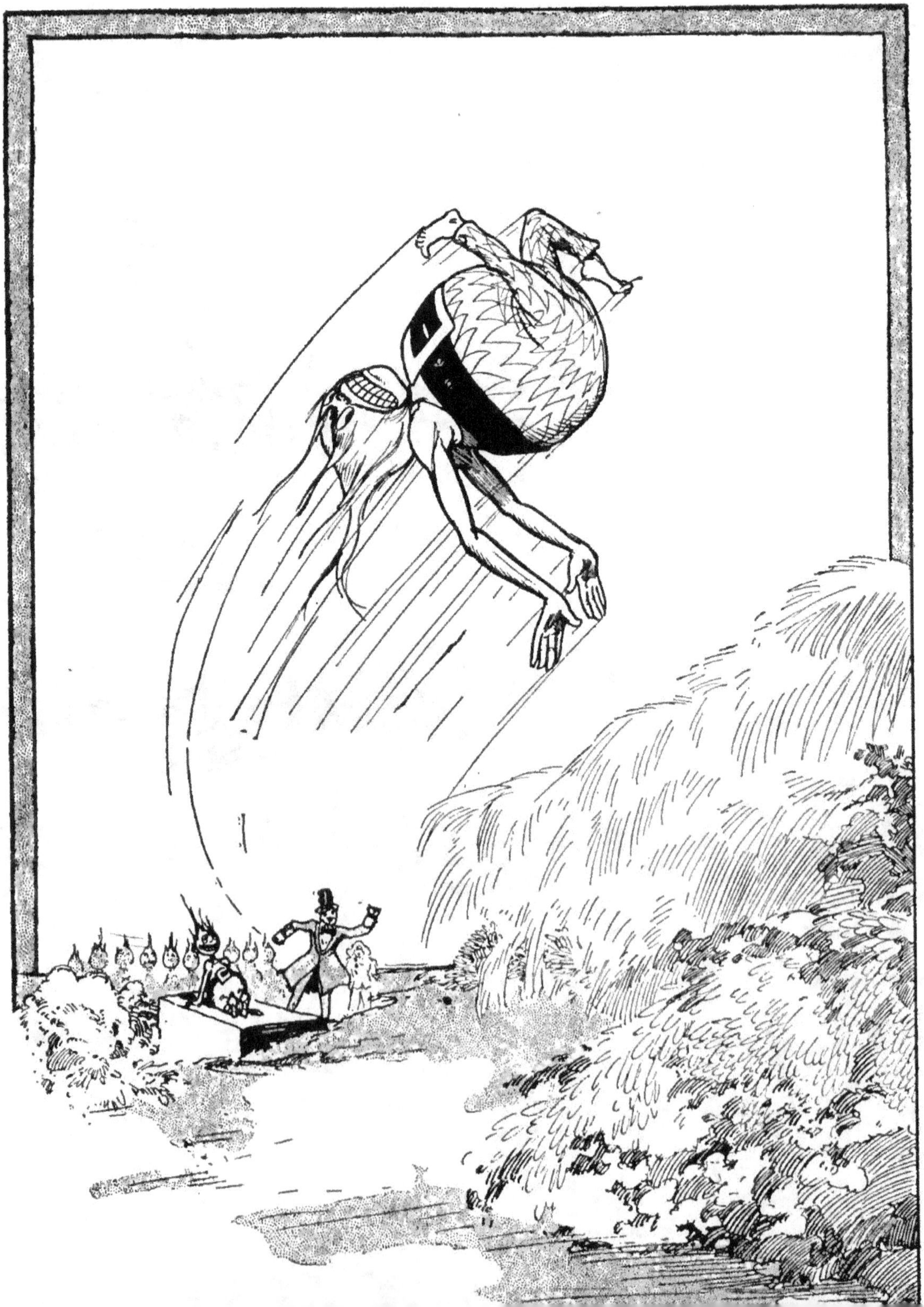

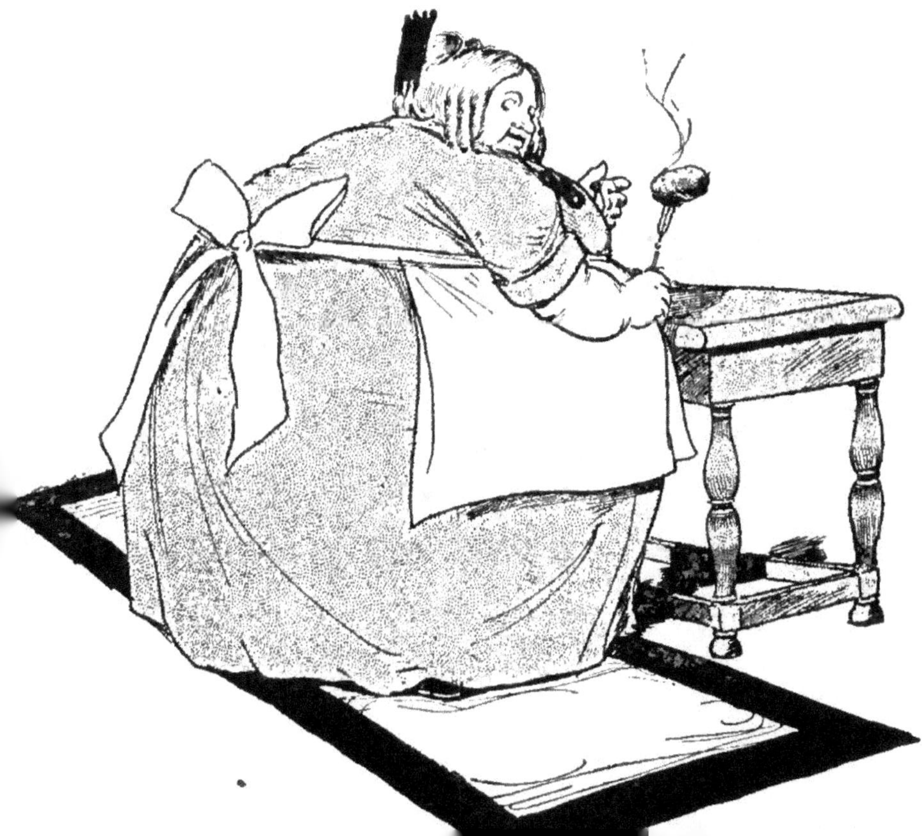

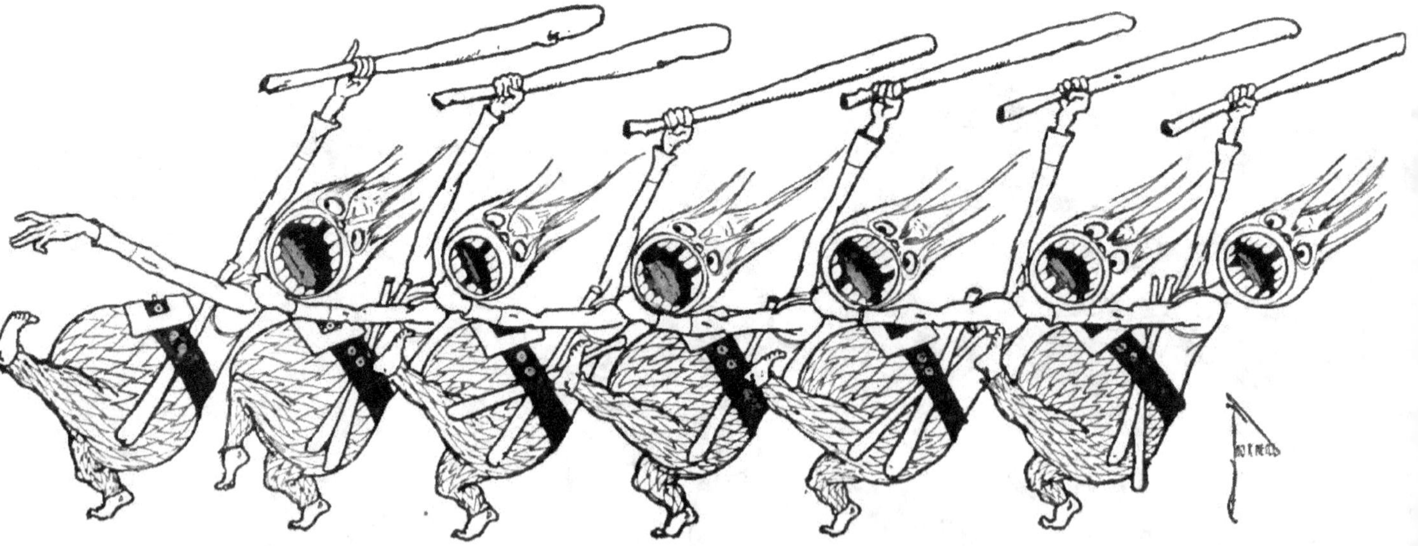

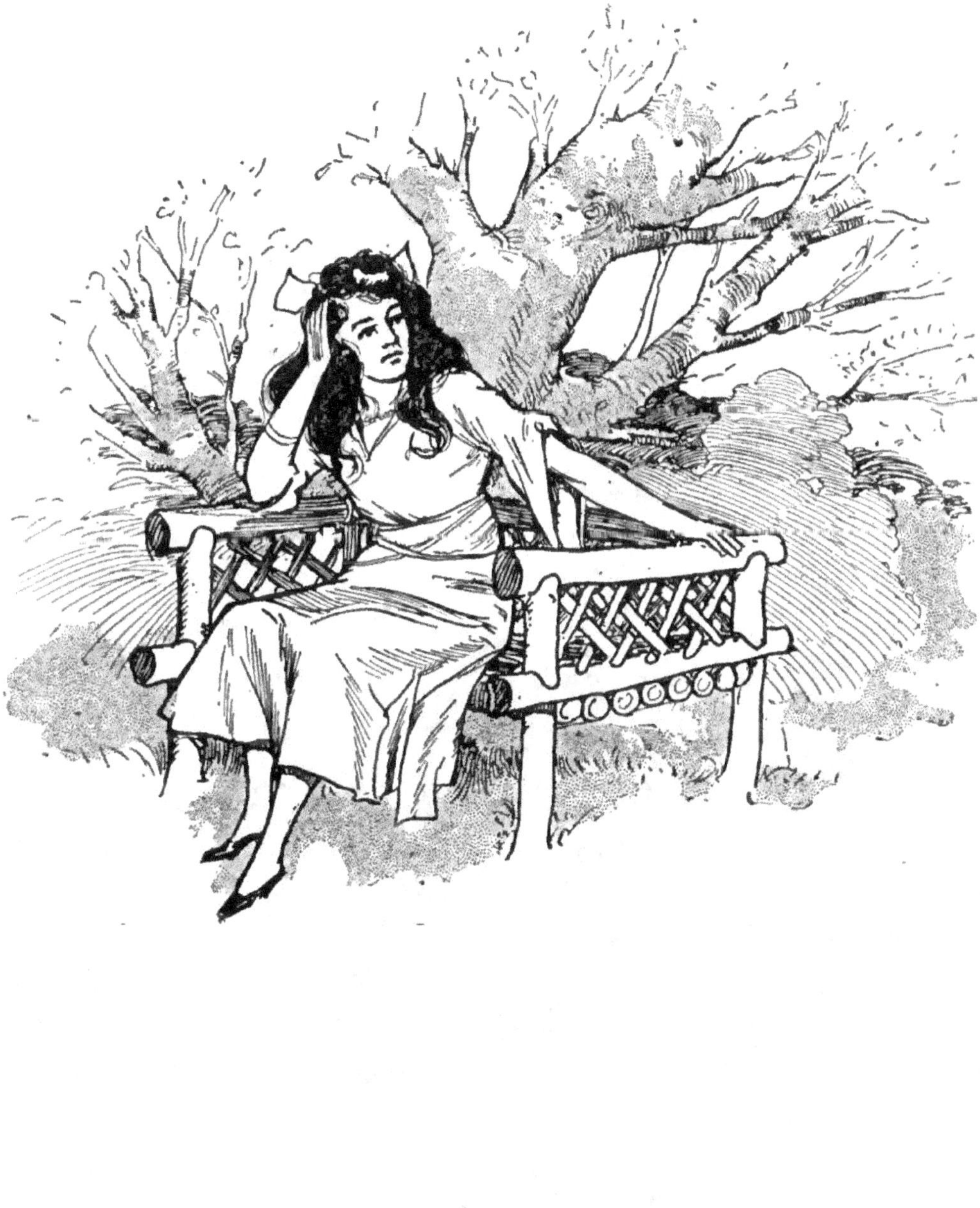

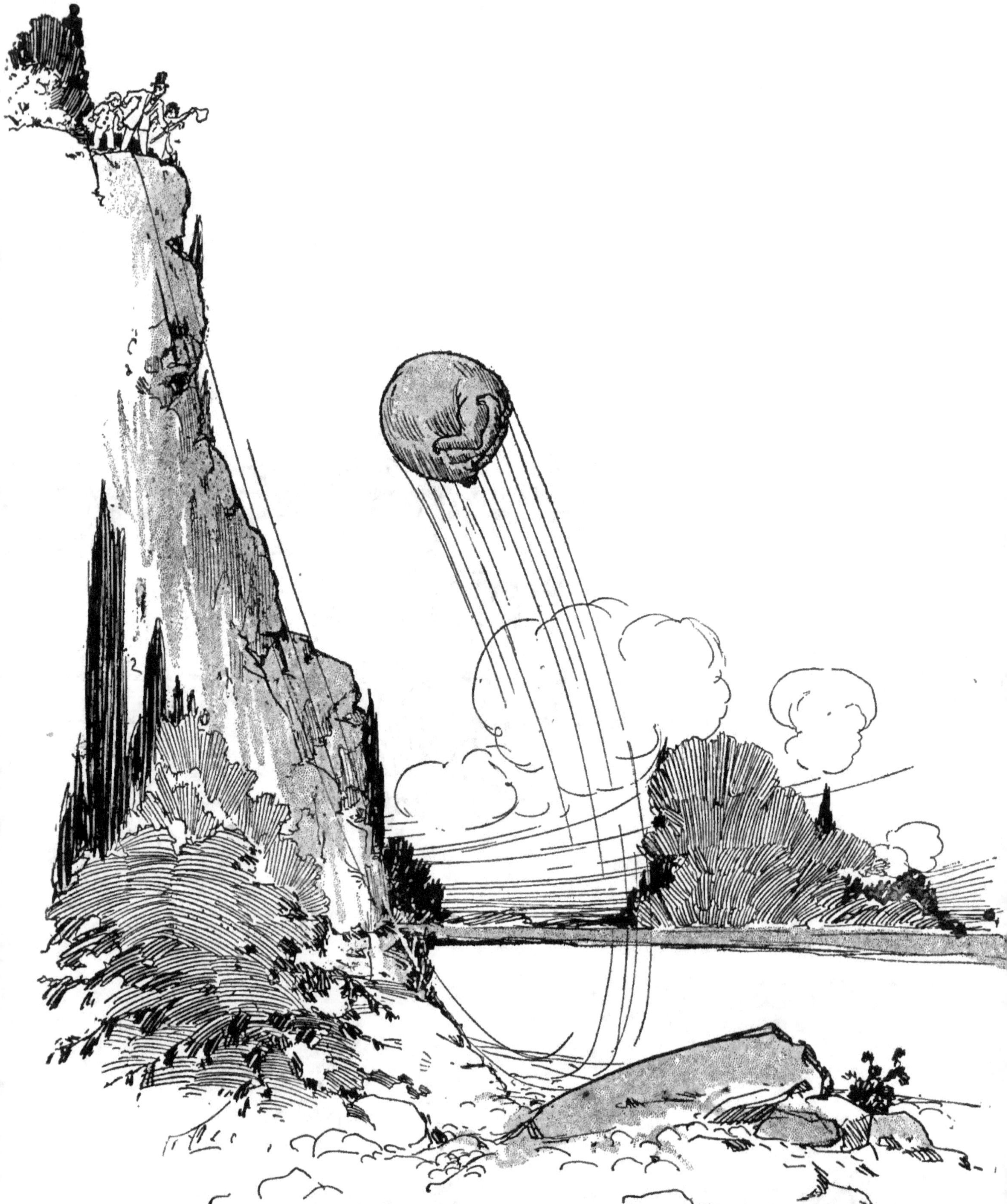

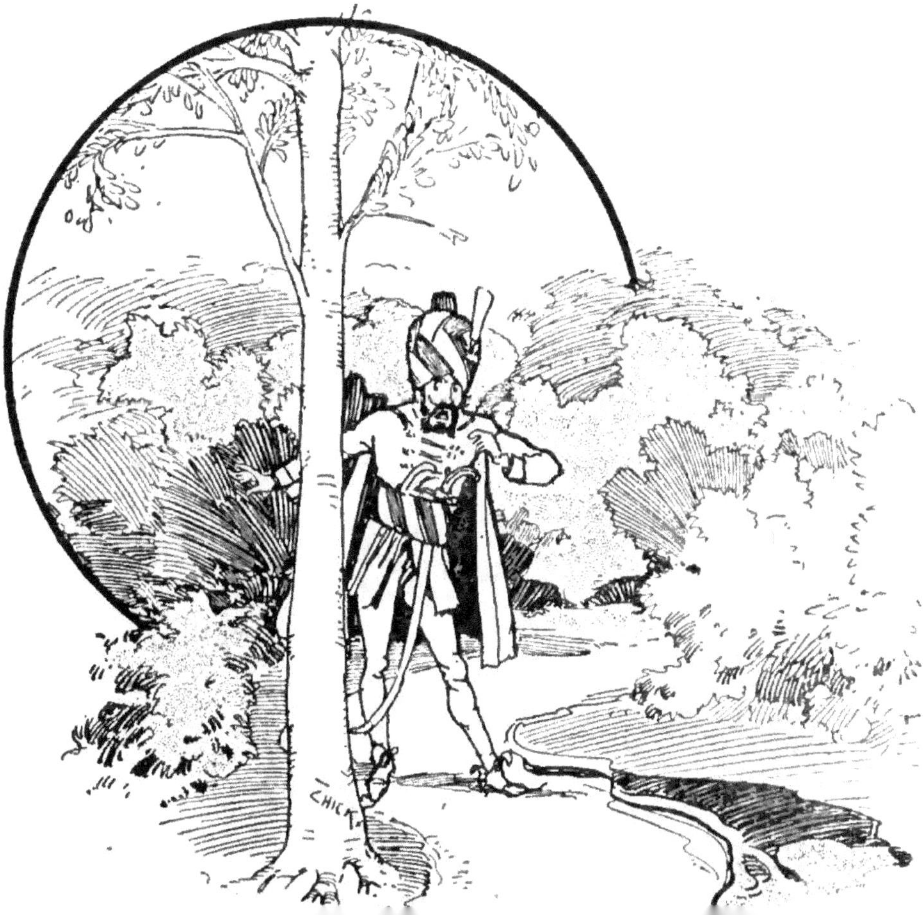
CHICK

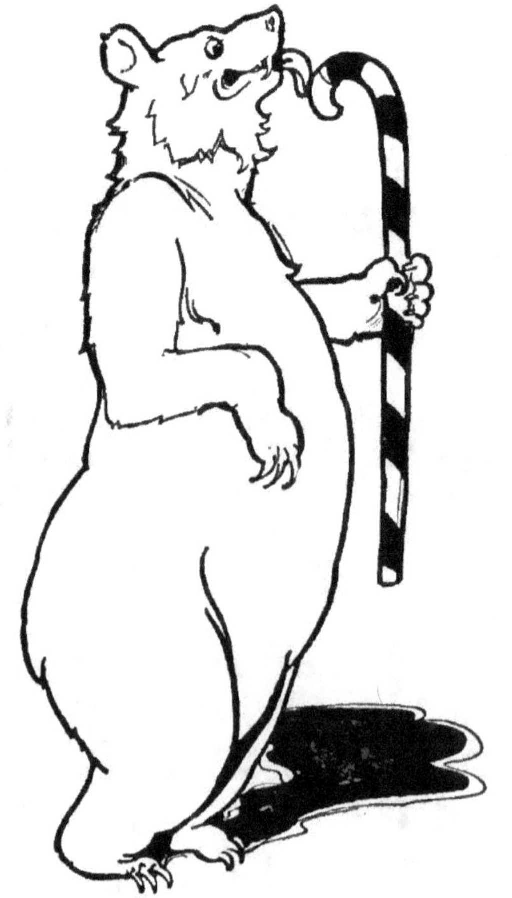

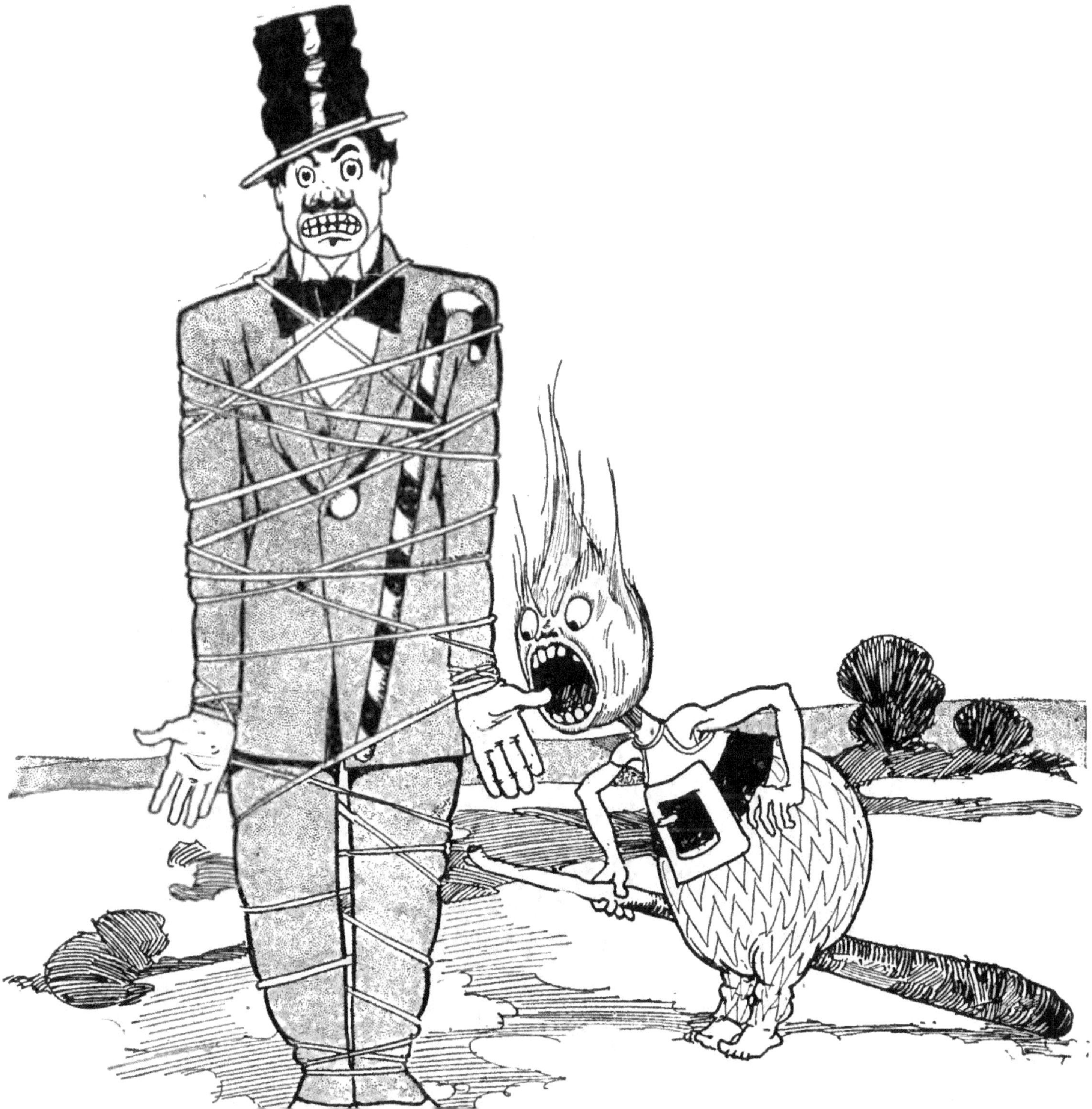

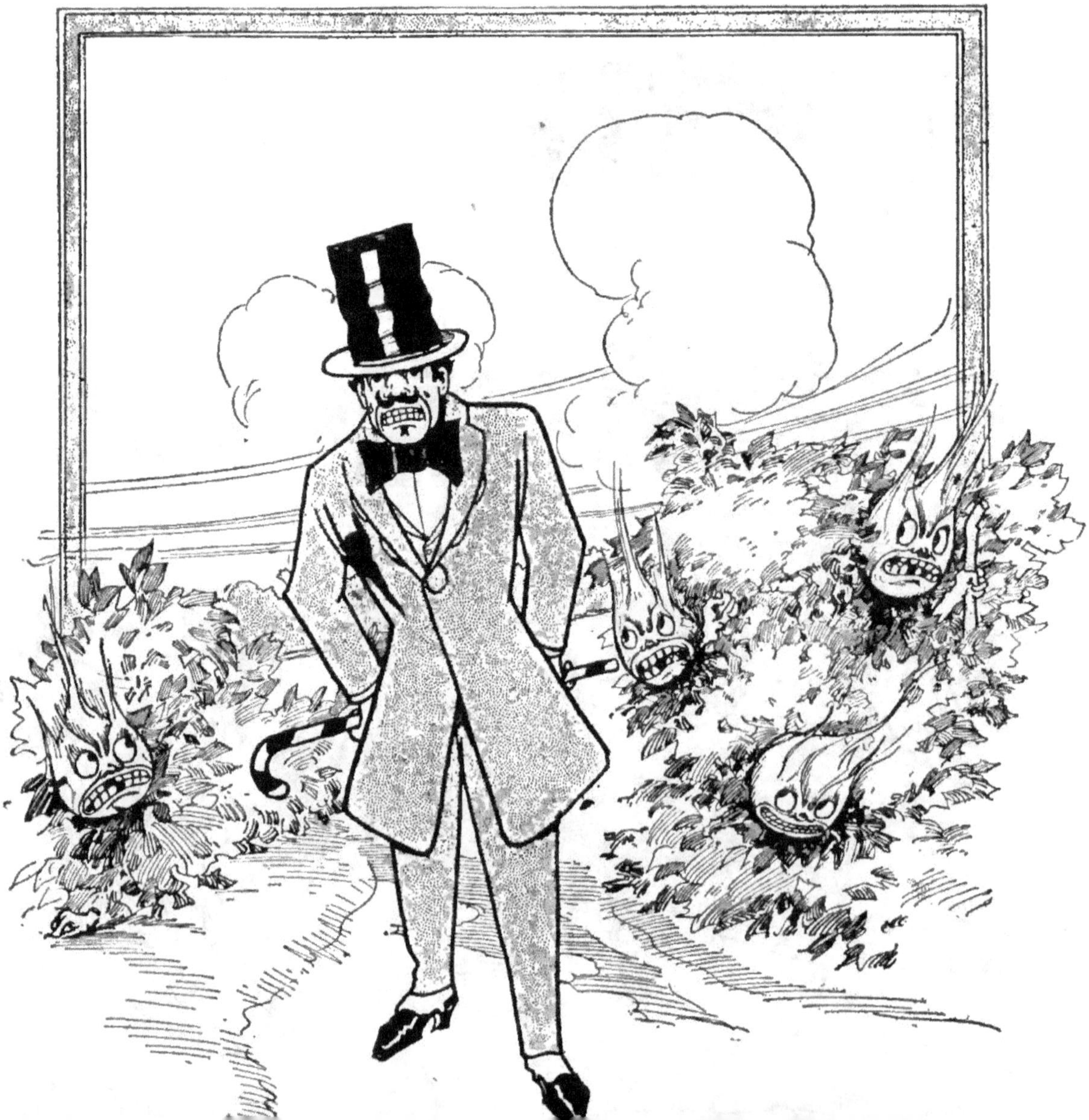

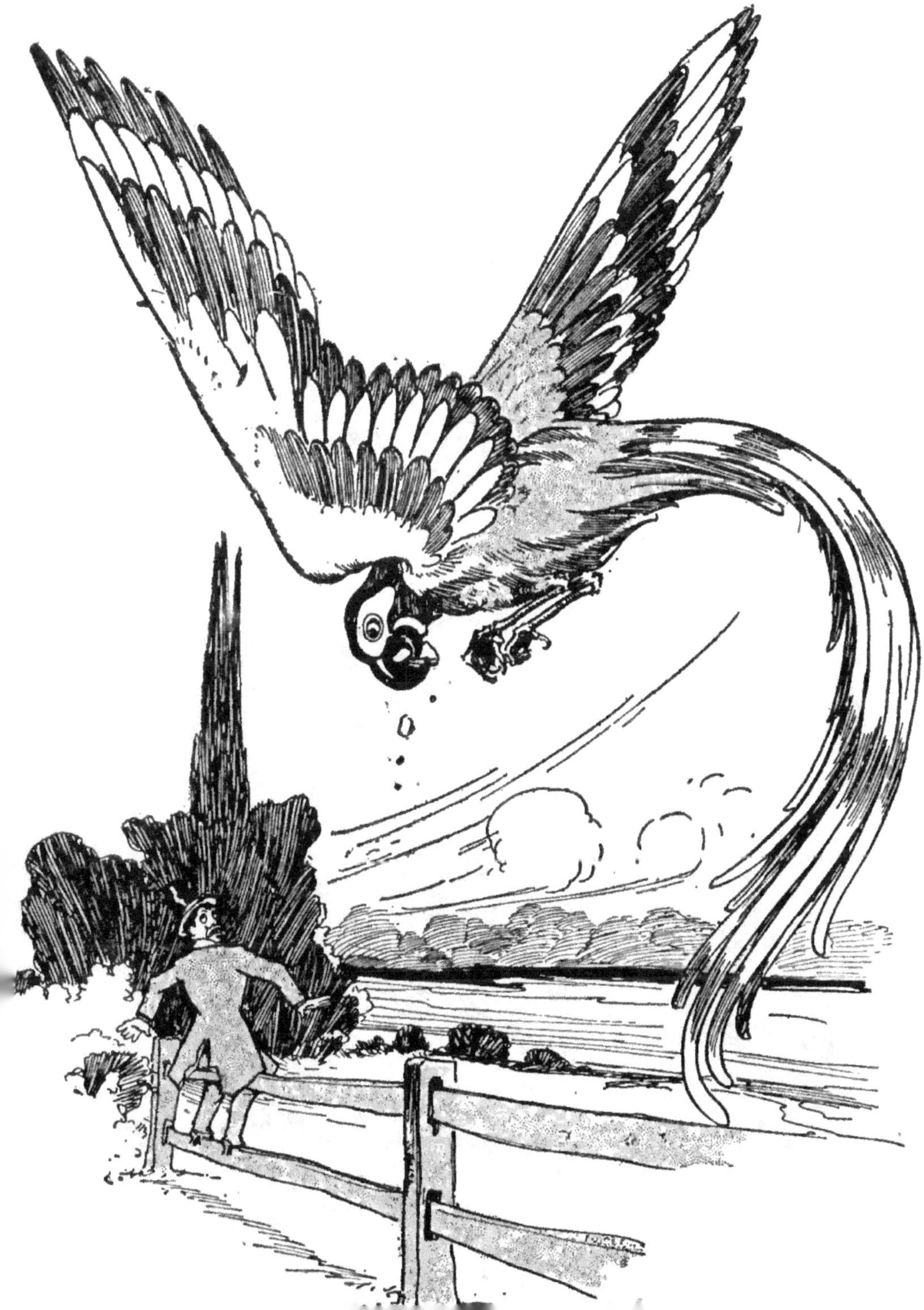

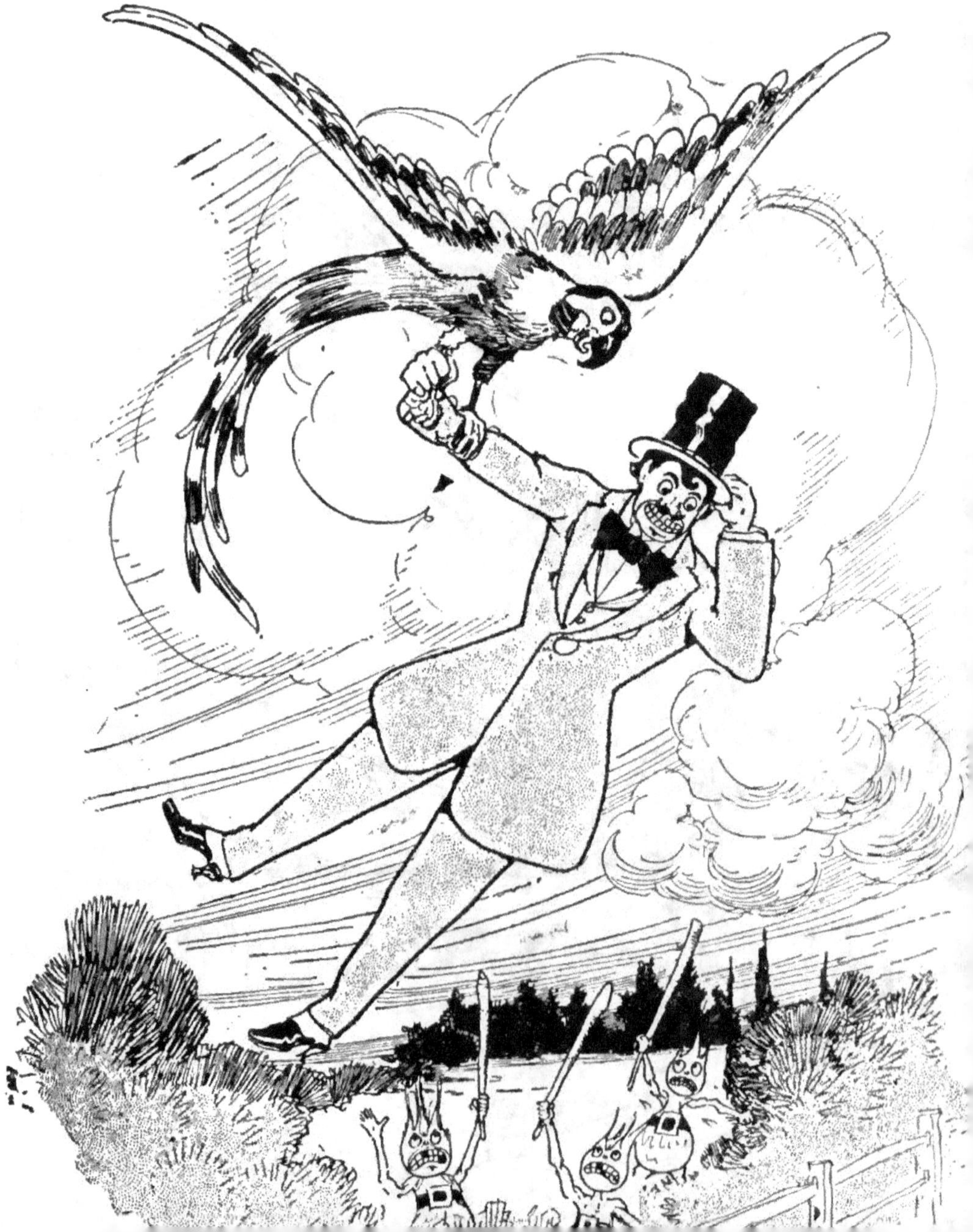

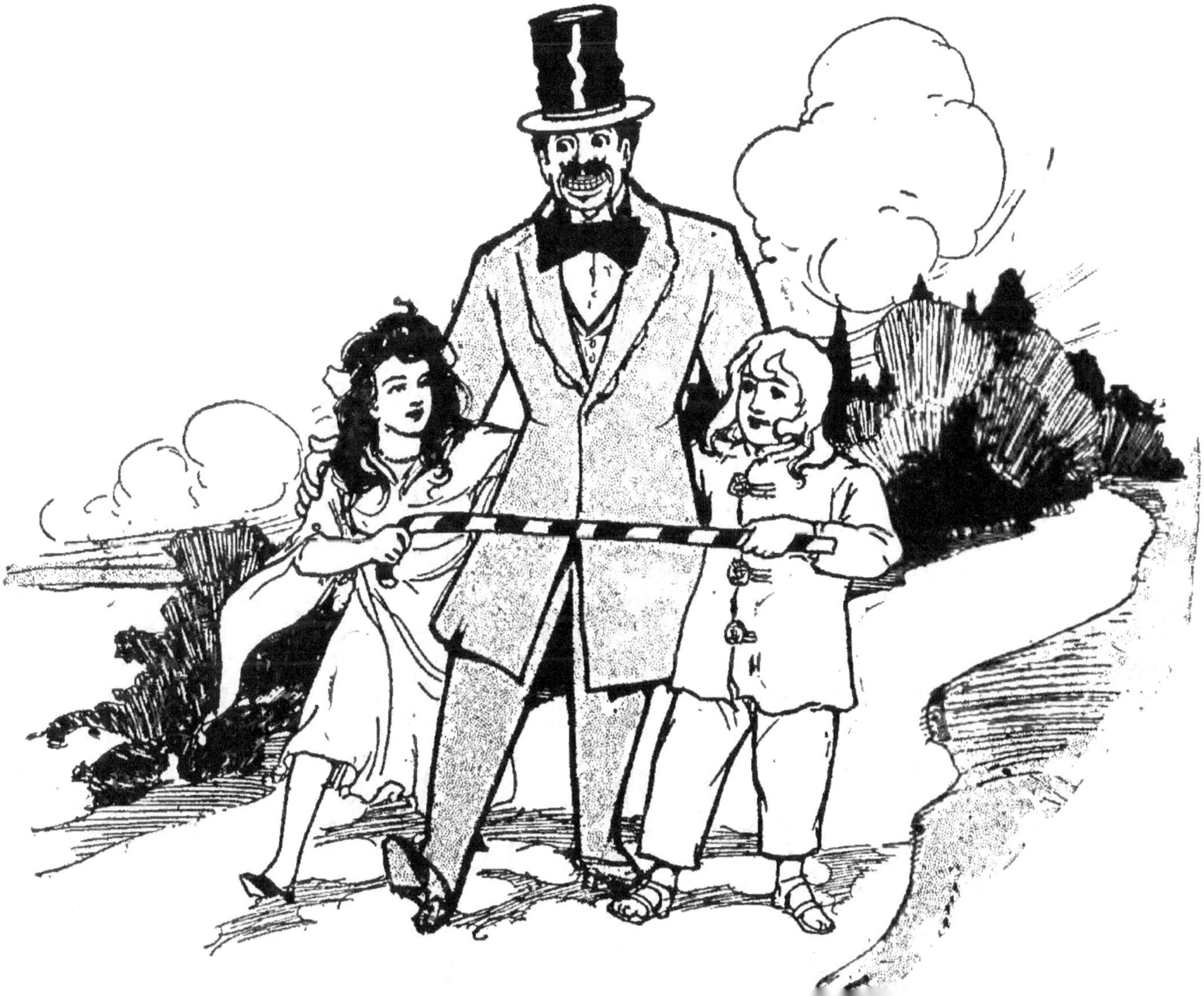

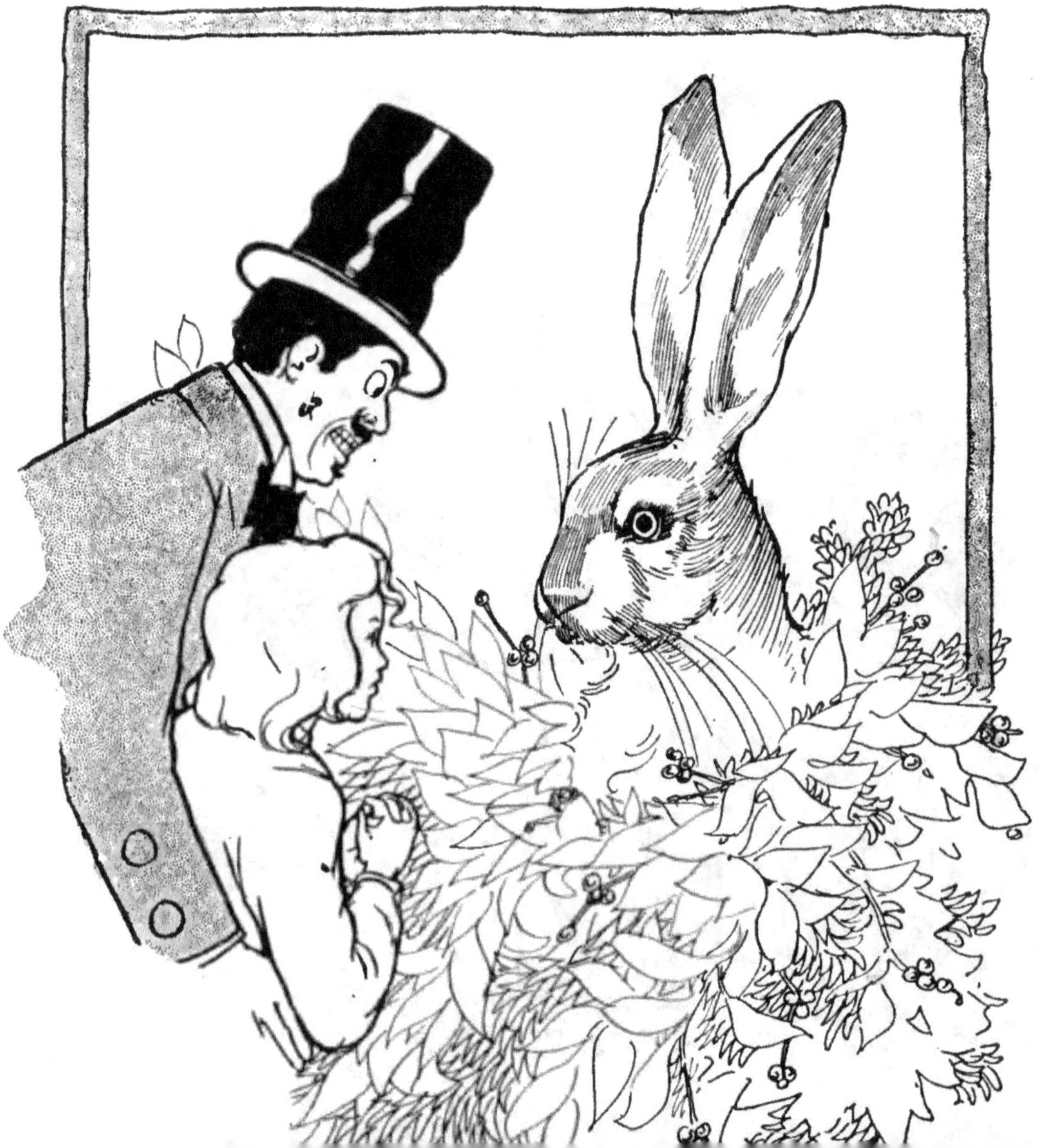

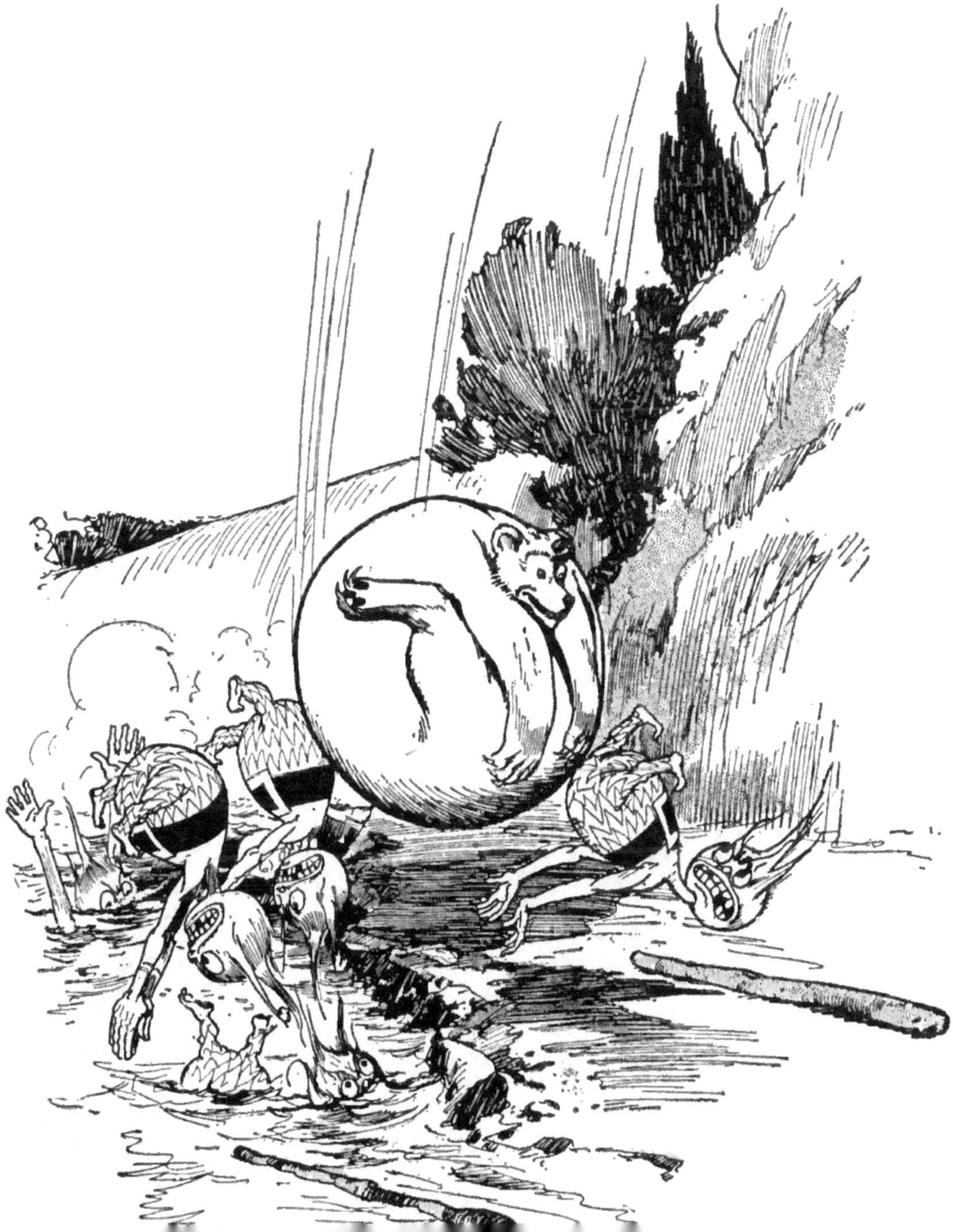

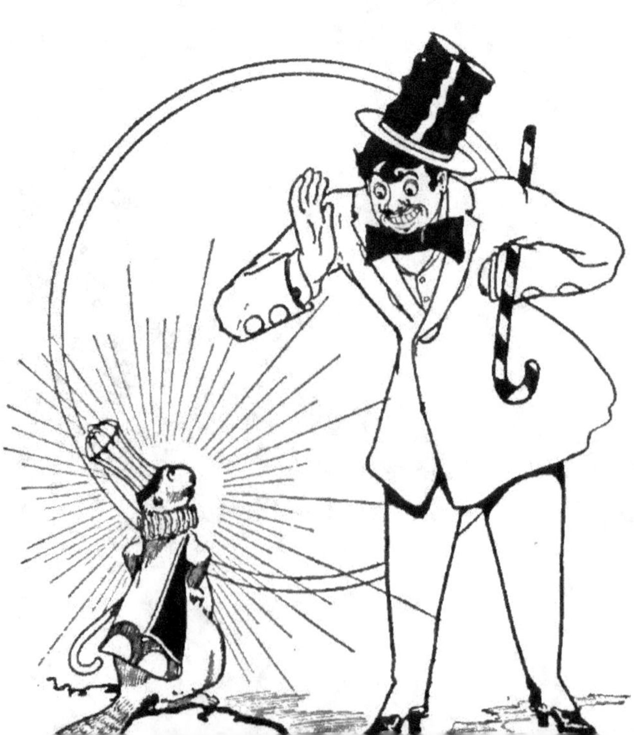

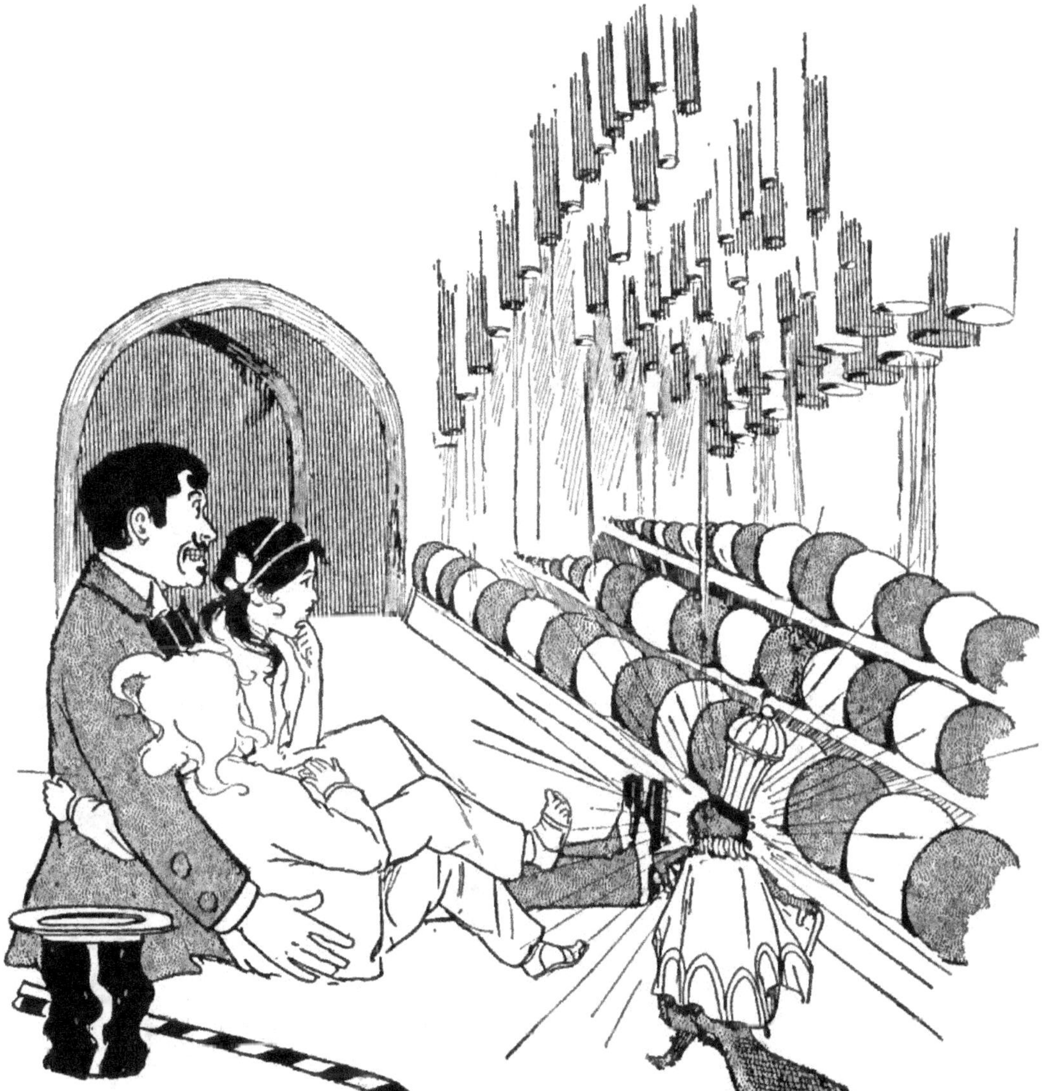

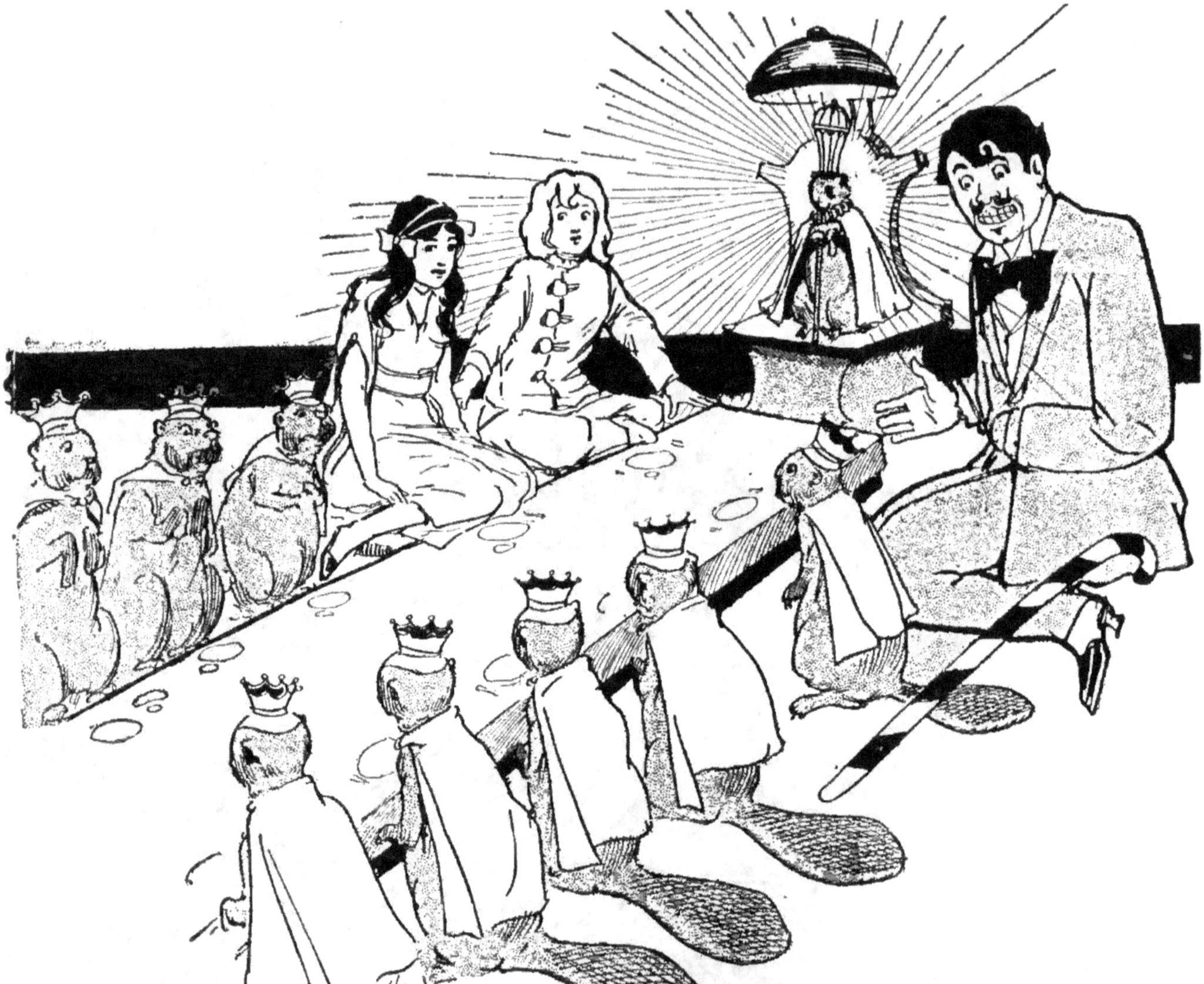

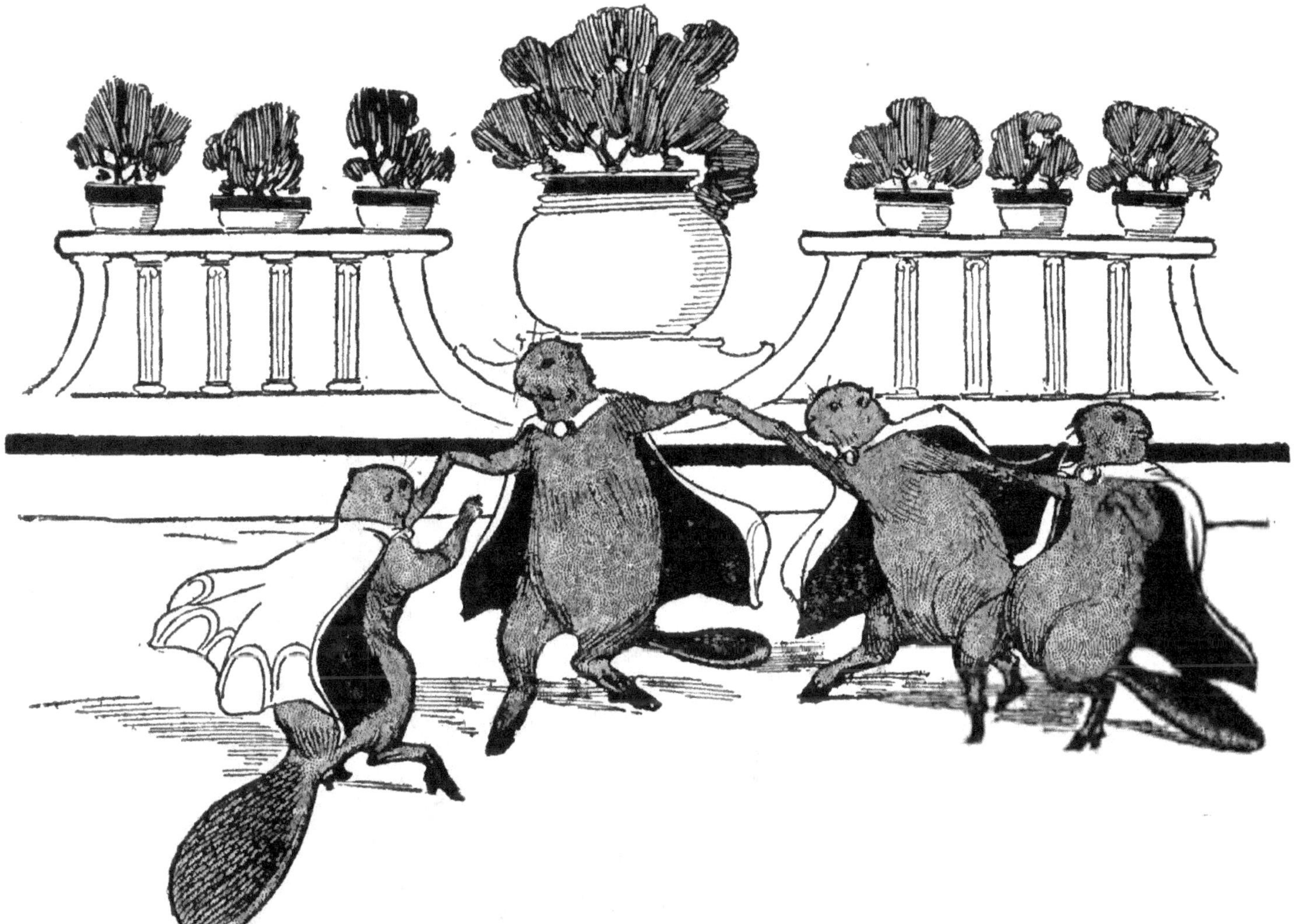

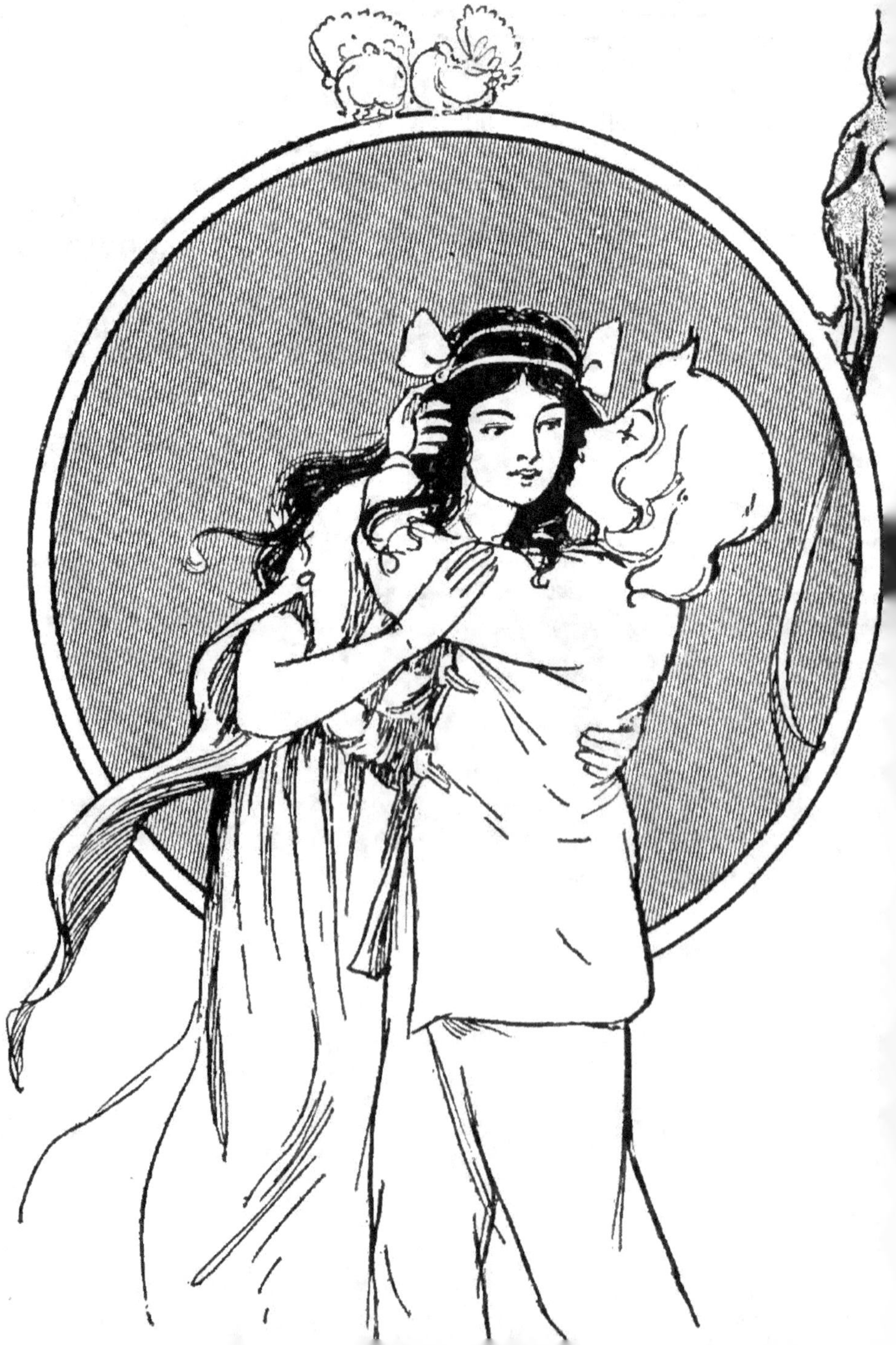

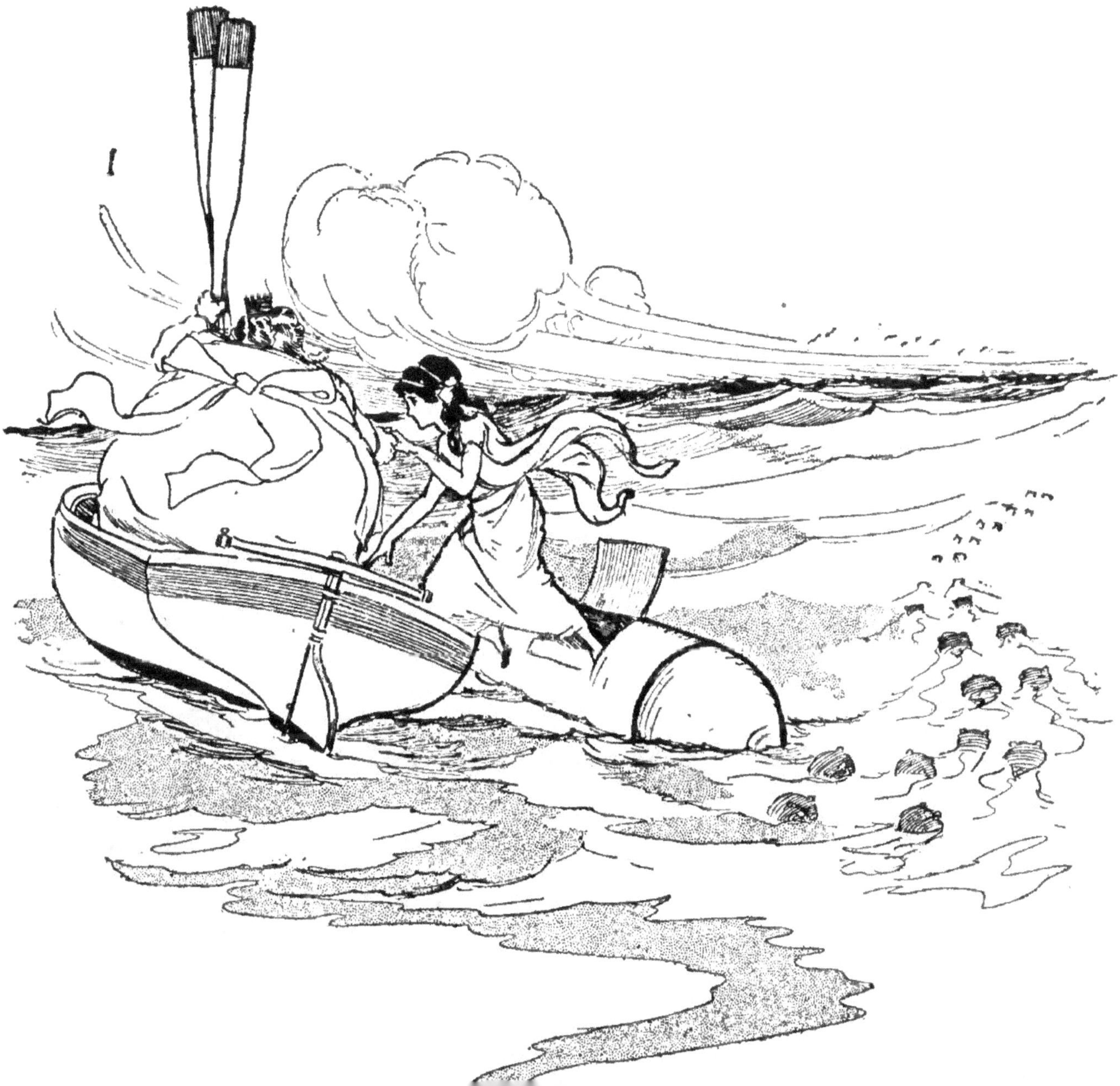

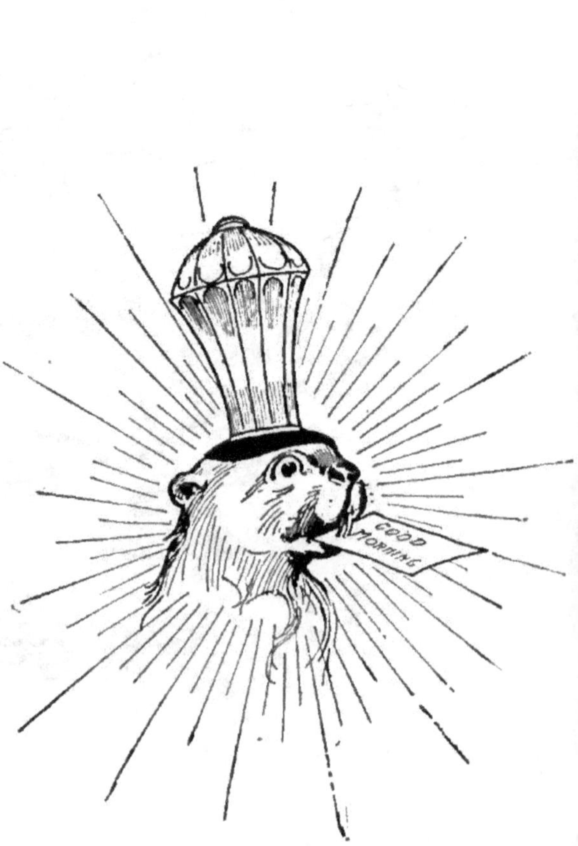
GOOD
MORNING

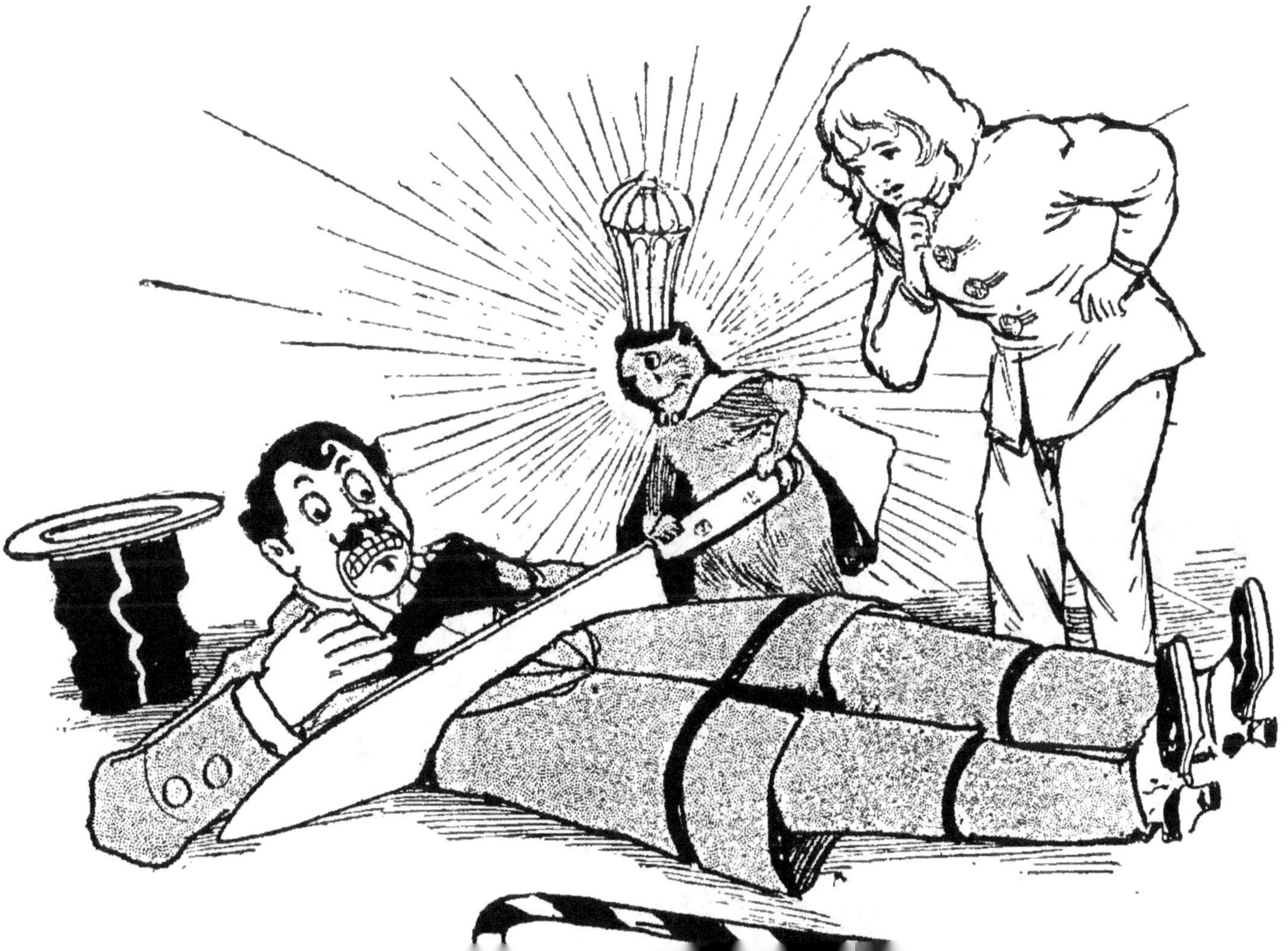

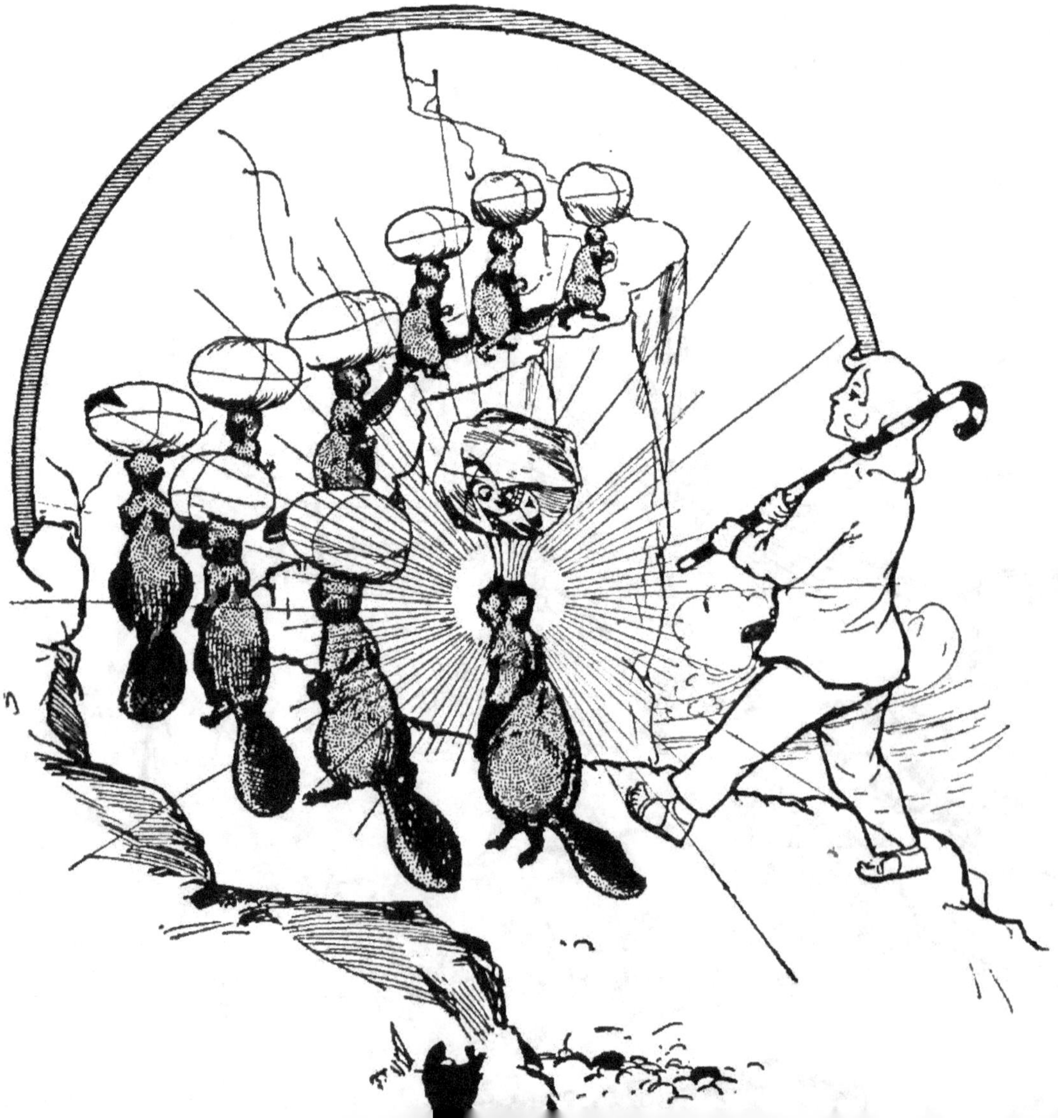

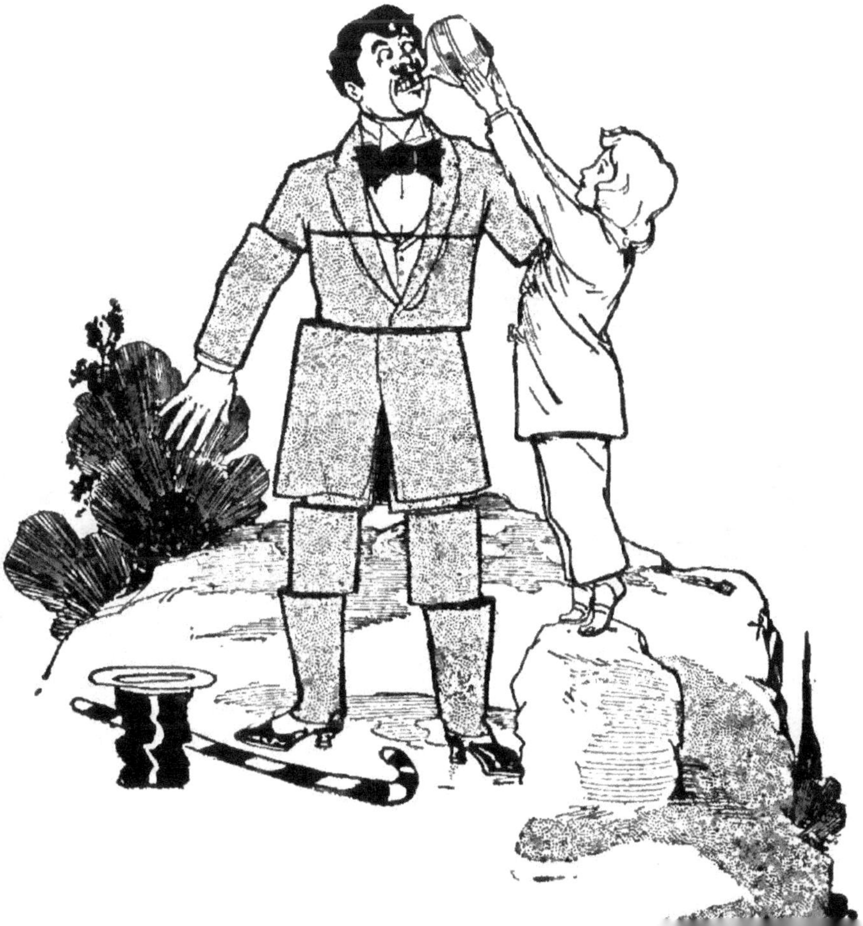

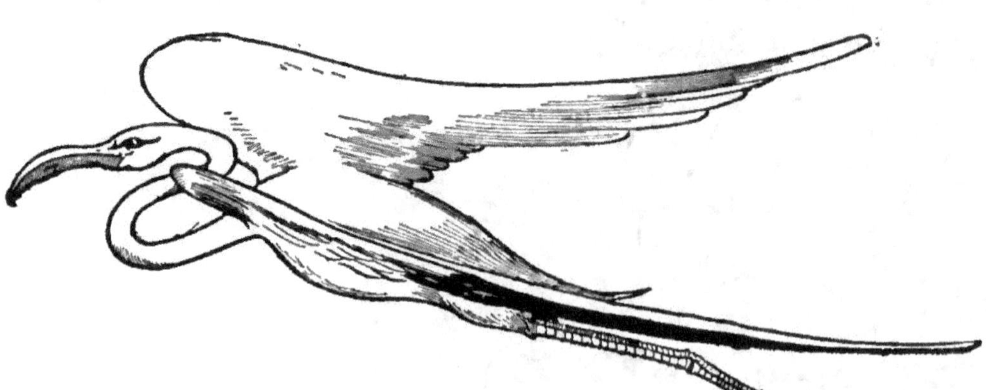

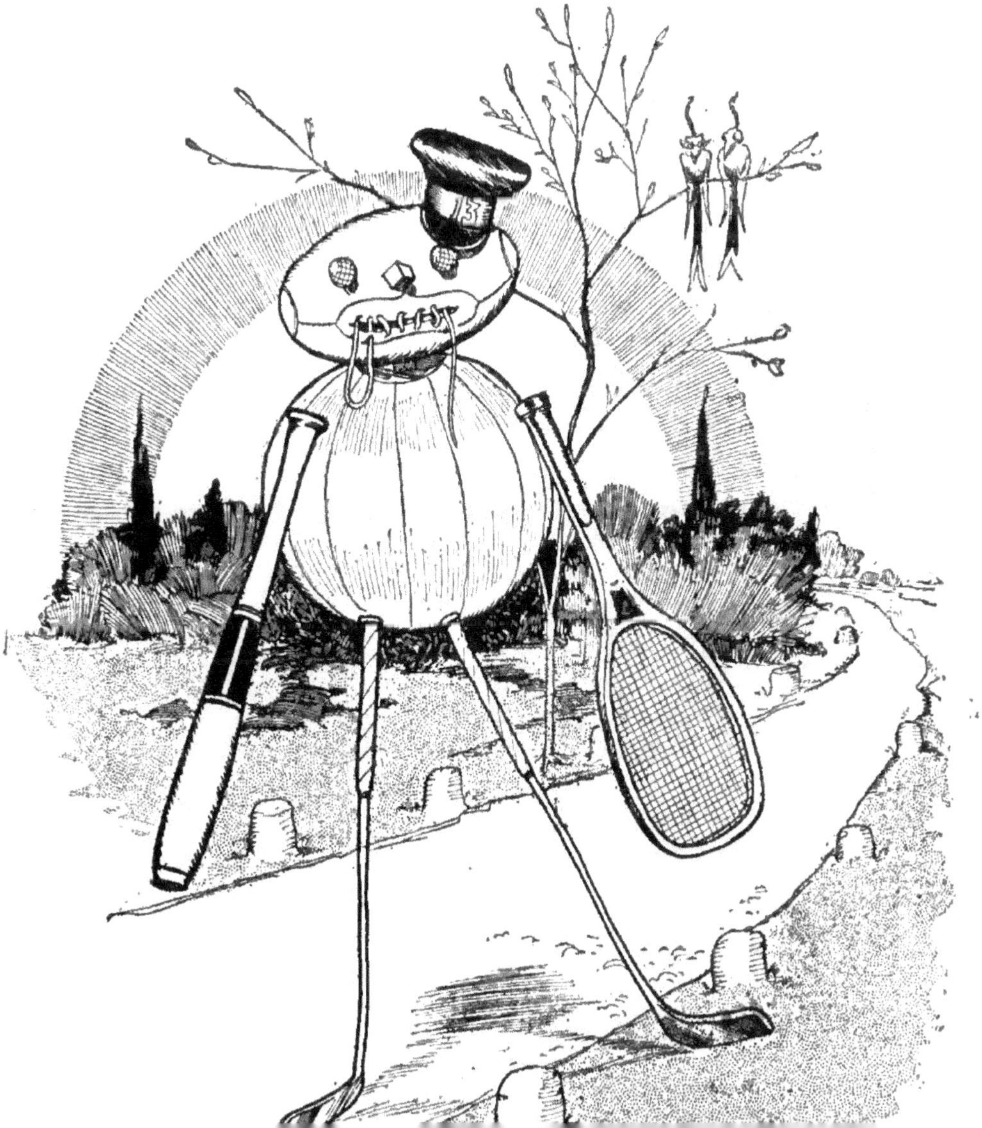

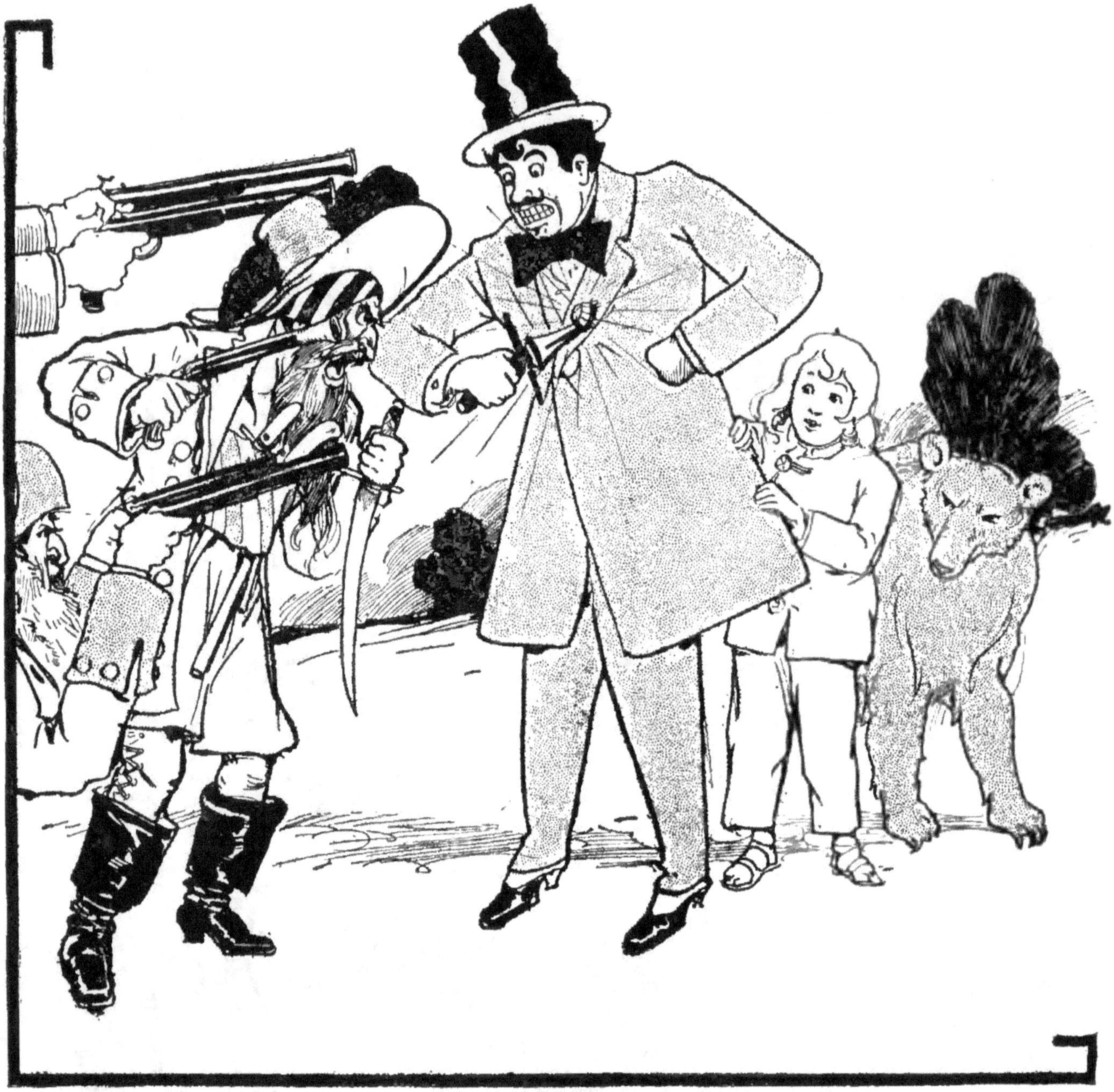

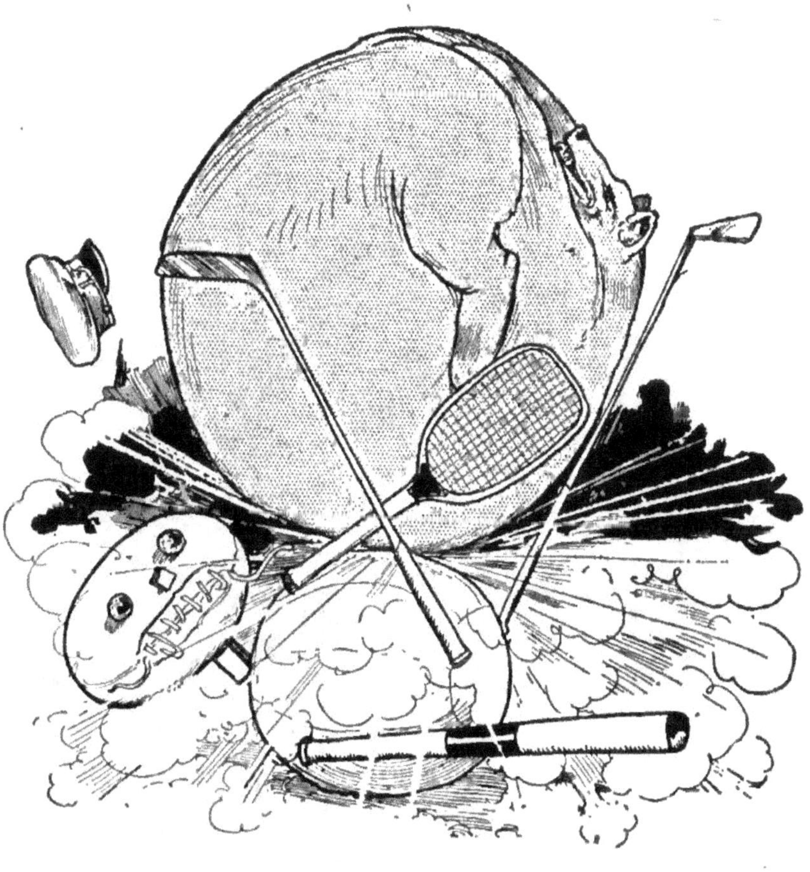

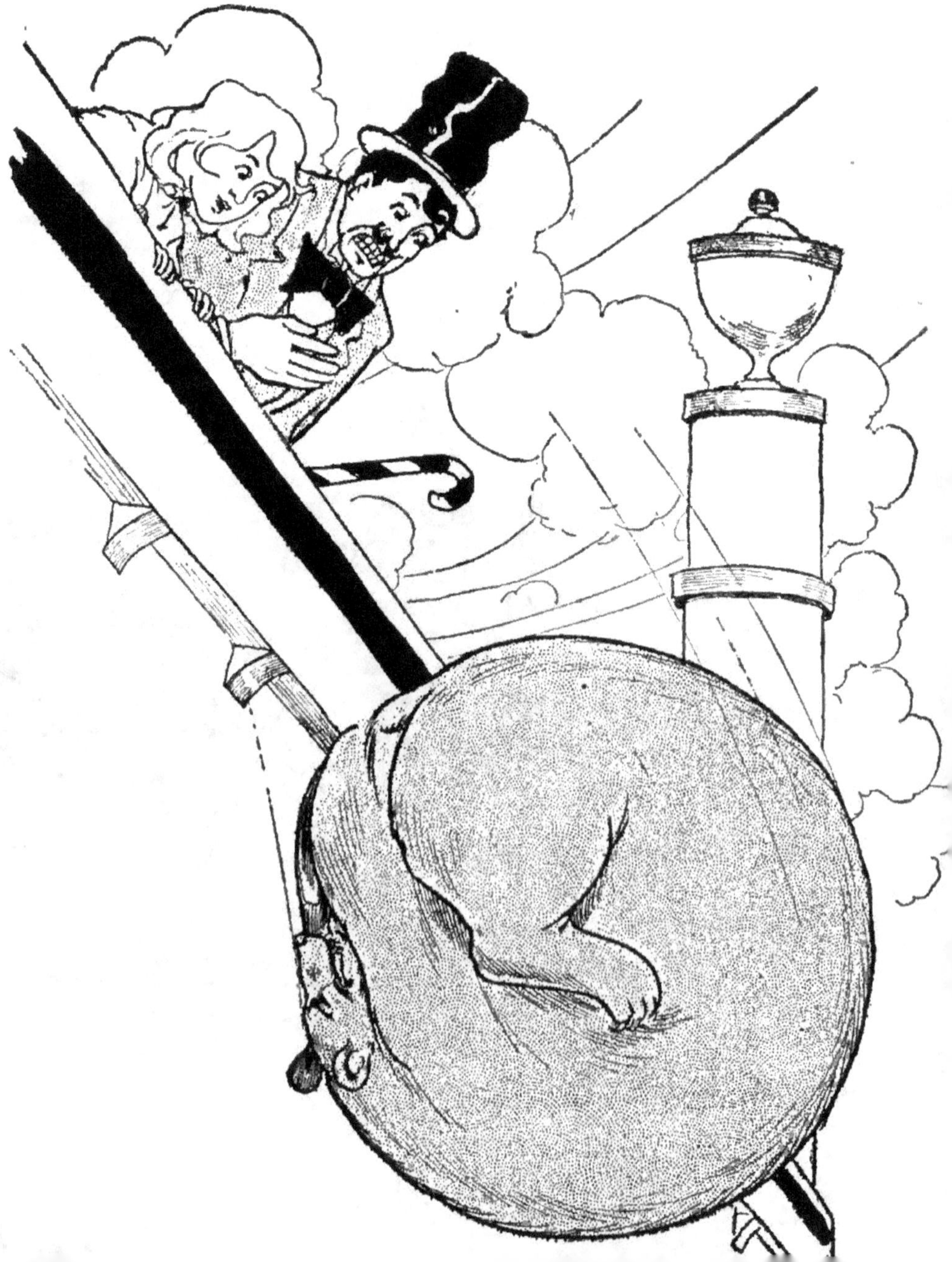

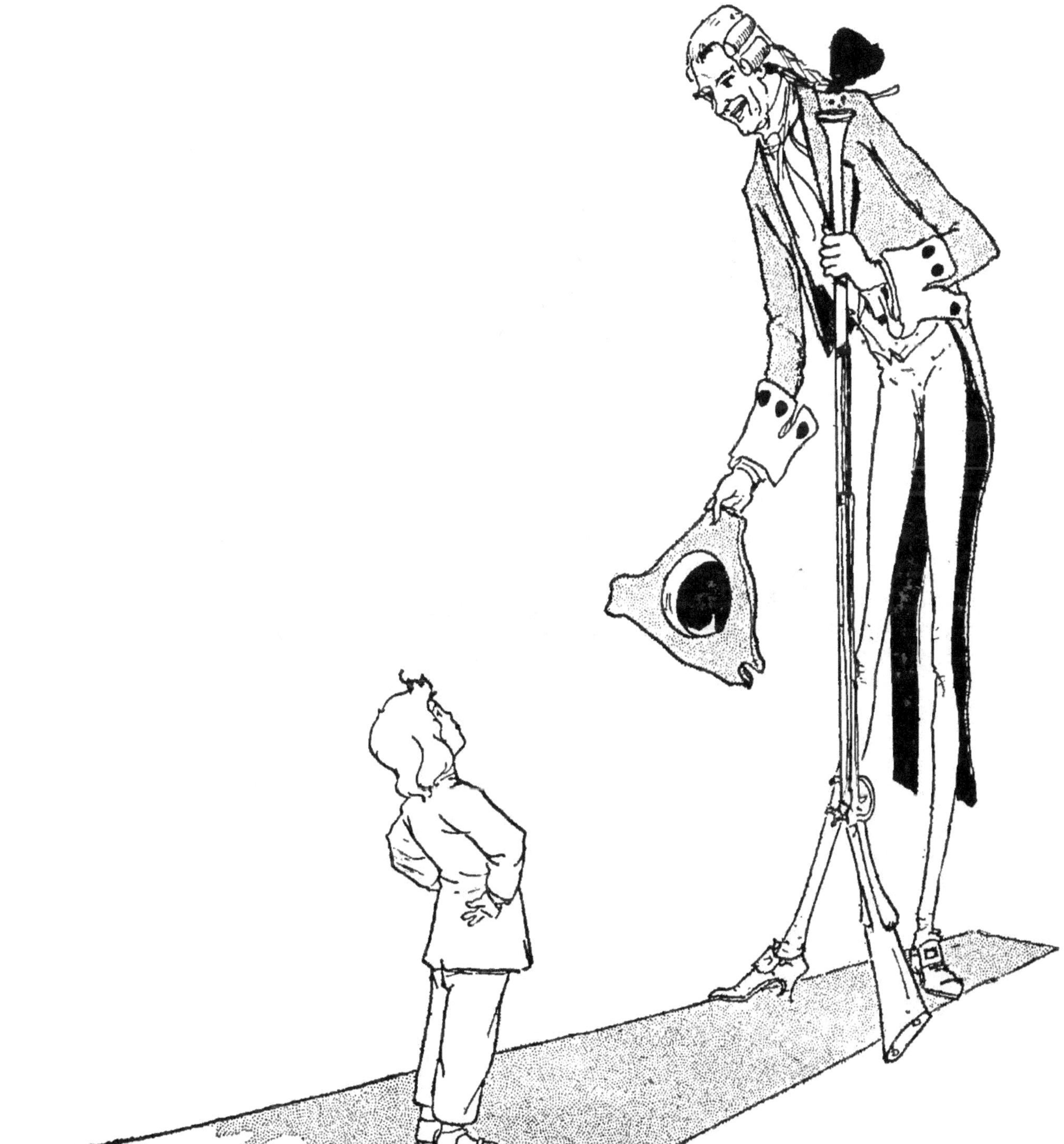

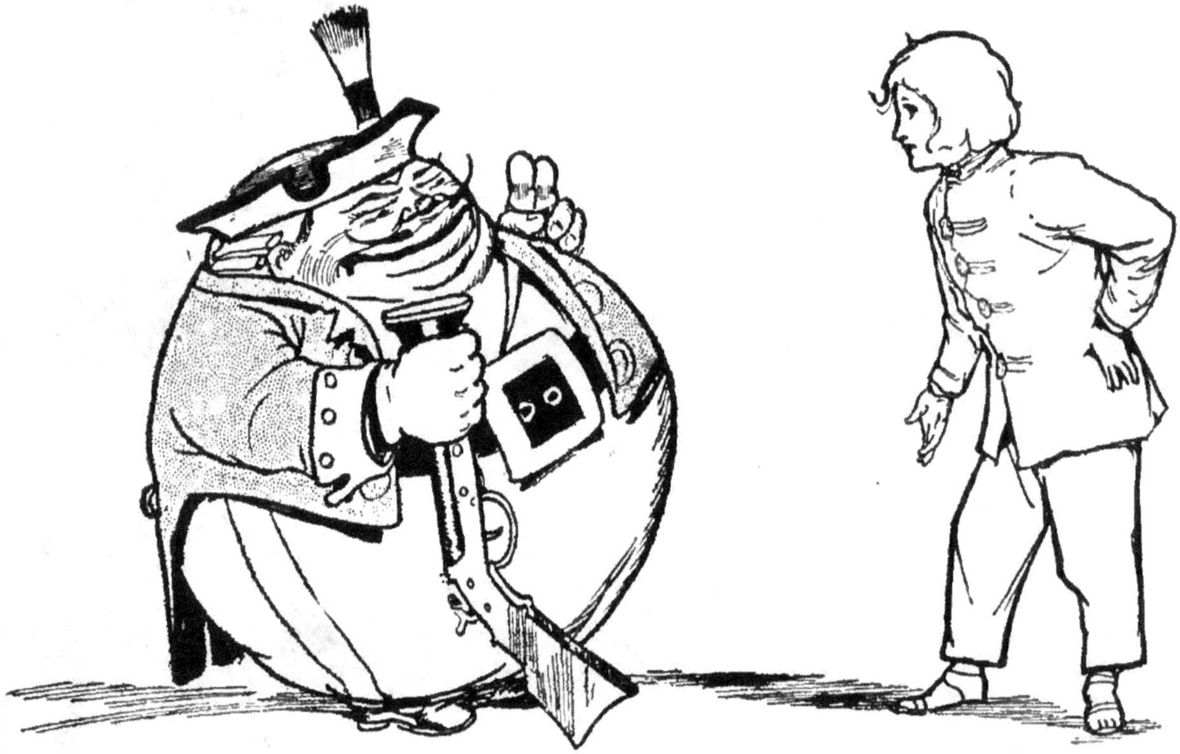

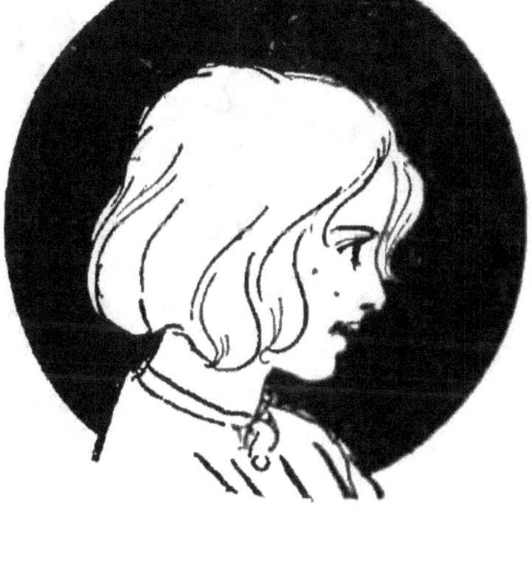

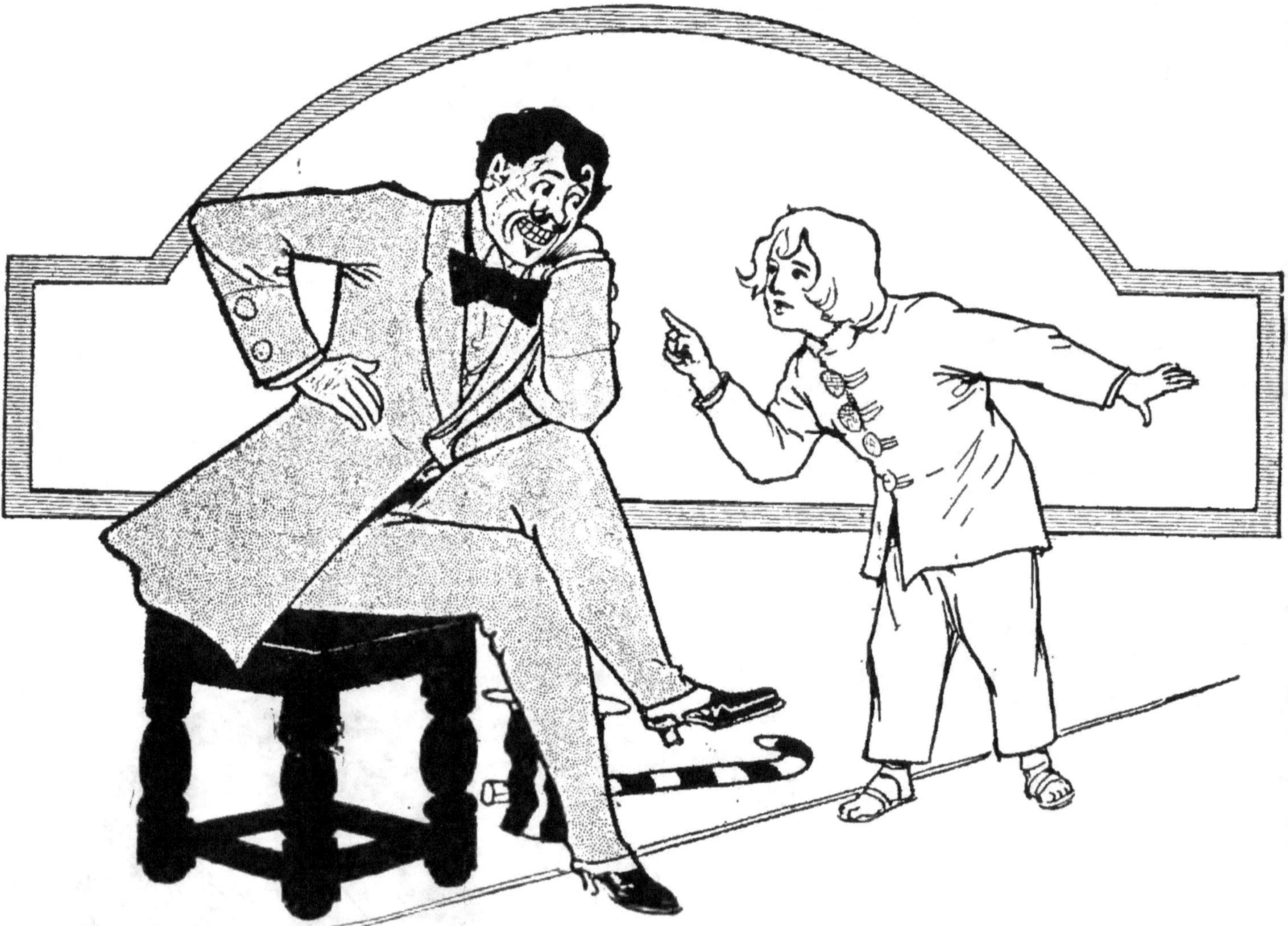

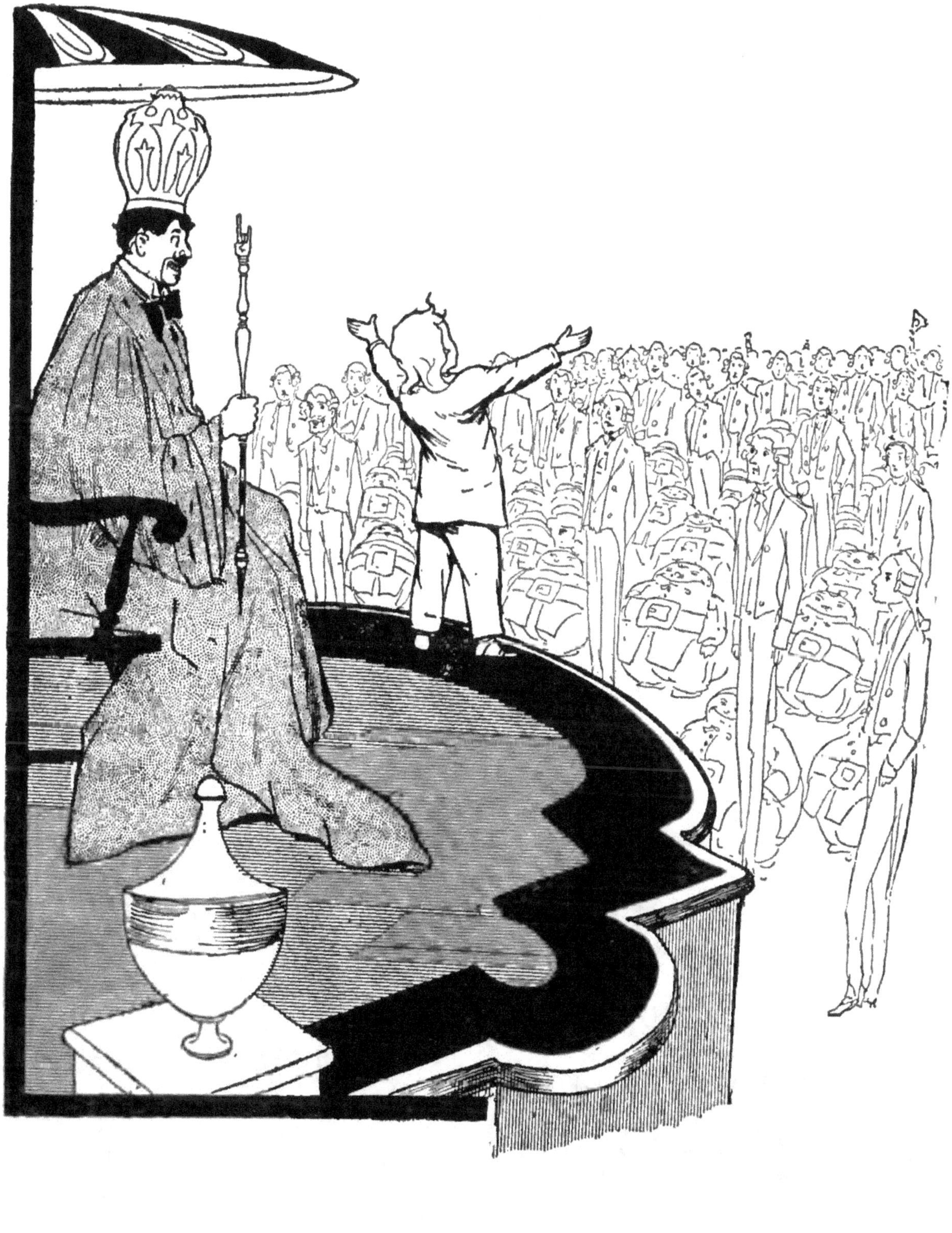

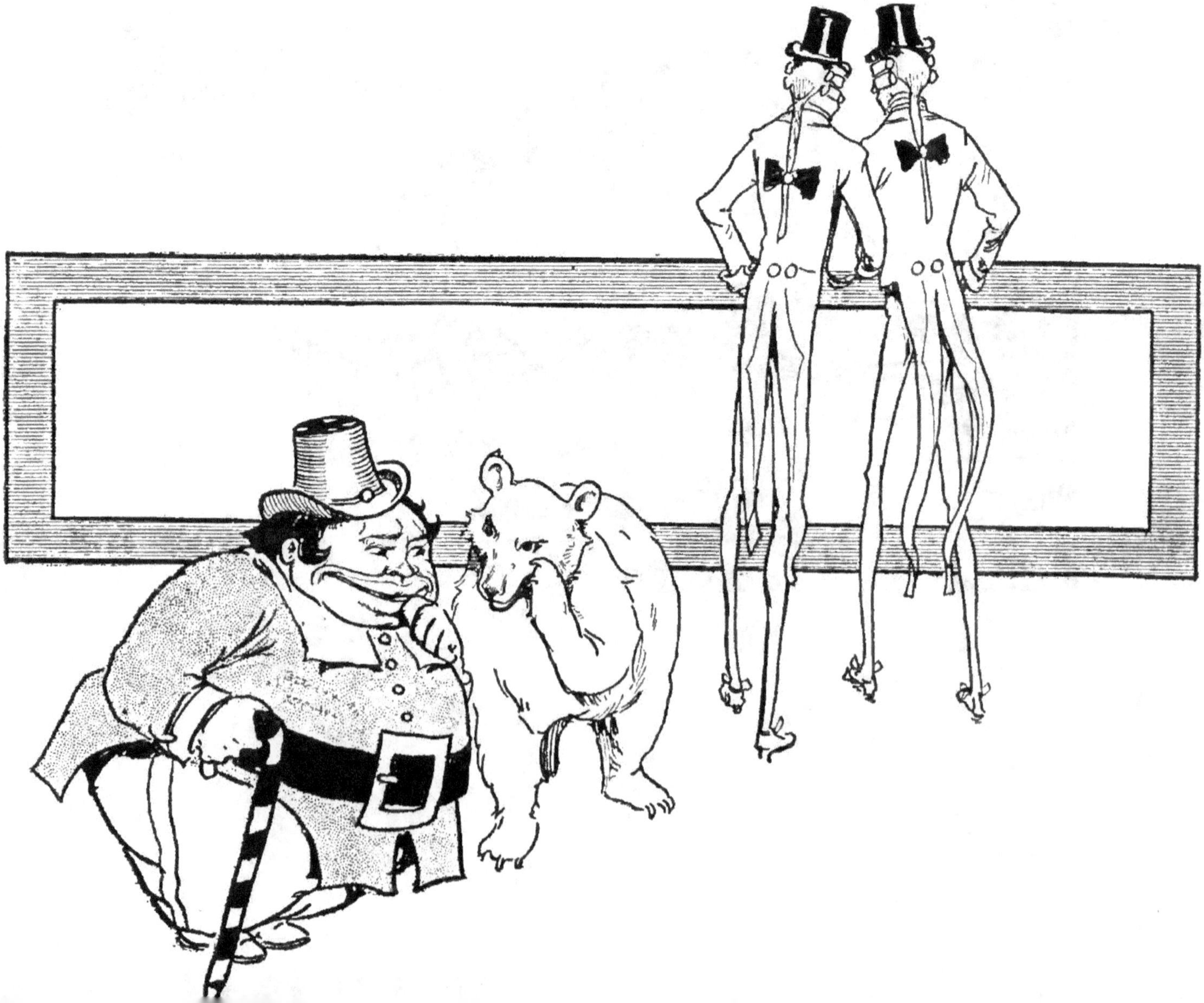

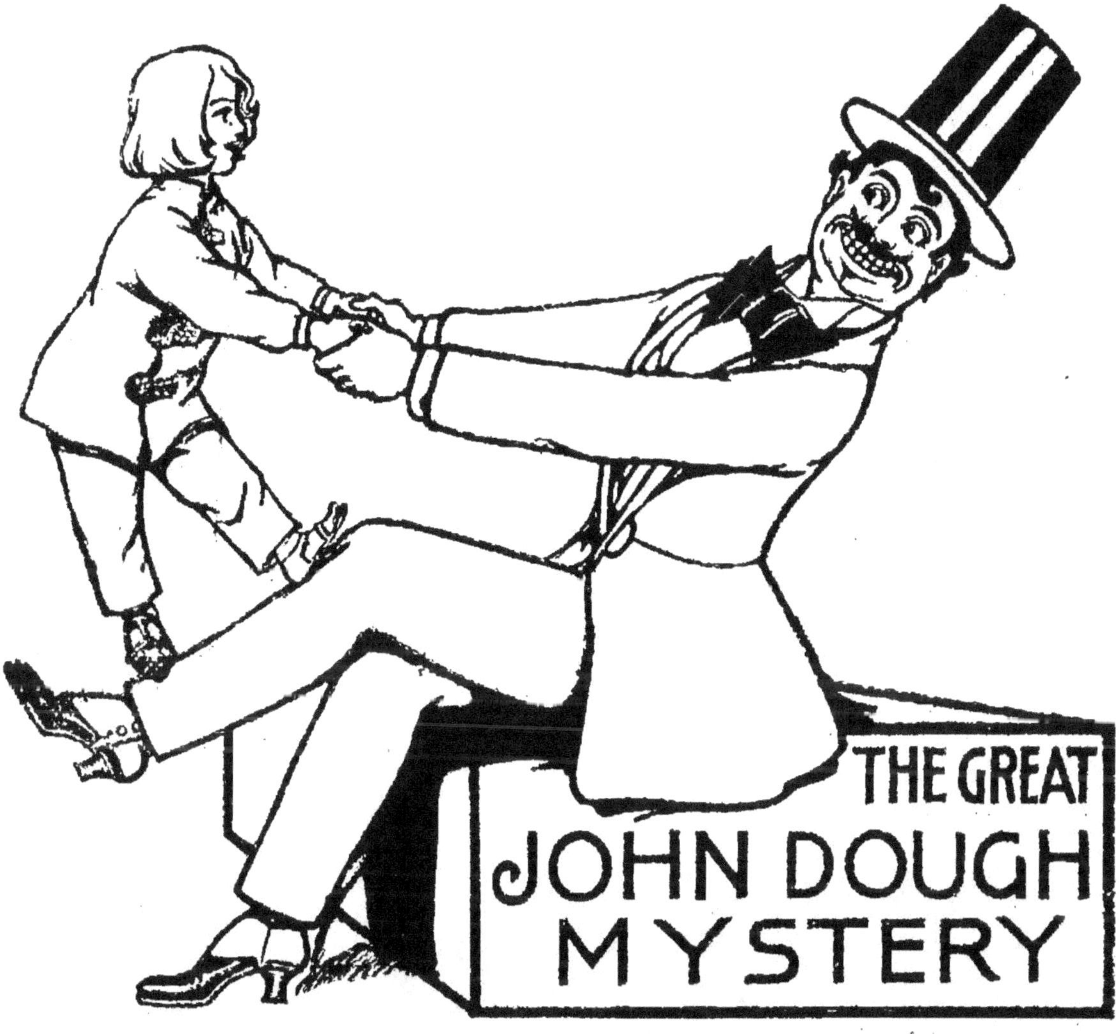
THE GREAT
JOHN DOUGH
MYSTERY

www.ingramcontent.com/pod-product-compliance
Lightning Source LLC
Chambersburg PA
CBHW081119180526
45170CB00008B/2912